5387 XB-70A FIRST FLIGHT 21 SEP 64

XB-70
Valkyrie

Jeannette Remak and Joe Ventolo Jr.

BUILDING NO.
307

MBI Publishing Company

Dedication

To Major Carl S. Cross, USAF; and Mr. Joseph A. Walker,
NASA; and to all test pilots, everywhere.

First published in 1998 by MBI Publishing Company, 729 Prospect Avenue, PO Box 1, Osceola, WI 54020-0001 USA

MBI Publishing Company books are also available at discounts in bulk quantity for industrial or sales-promotional use. For details write to Special Sales Manager at Motorbooks International Wholesalers & Distributors, 729 Prospect Avenue, Osceola, WI 54020-0001 USA.

Library of Congress Cataloging-in-Publication Data

Ventolo, Joseph A.
    XB-70 Valkyrie : the Ride to Valhalla / Joe Ventolo, Jr.
& Jeannette Remak.
        p.   cm.
        Includes index.
    ISBN 0-7603-0555-2 (pbk. : alk. paper)
    1. B-70 bomber—Design and construction—History.
2, High-speed aeronautics—Government policy—United States—History. 3. Aeronautics, Military—Research—Government policy—United States—History. I. Remak, Jeannette. II. Title.
    TL685.3.V46 1998
    623.7'463—dc21   98-37887

On the front cover: The XB-70 Valkyrie banks smoothly away to climb and accelerate to her operating altitude of more than 60,000 feet at Mach 3. *USAF Museum*

On the frontispiece: Like a spacecraft from another planet, XB-70 AV-1 looks positively otherworldly in this photo. Those who witnessed her advanced materials and high performance might even be convinced it were true, as she was truly unique. *AFMC/HO*

On the title page: This photo provides a good look at the XB-70's windshield and nose ramp arrangement, which offered the best of both worlds by retracting down for better visibility during low speed flight, and pivoting up for better aerodynamics at high speed. *AFMC/HO*

On the back cover, top: No one had ever seen anything like her. Here, the XB-70 amazes the world and captures the media's attention as she rolls out into the public eye at North American Aviation. *USAF Museum*

On the back cover, bottom: The XB-70's enormous main landing gear bogie and strut. Note the smaller wheel, which is a sensor or wheelspin measuring device for controlling brake actuation, or anti-skid functions. *USAF Museum*

Printed in Hong Kong through World Print, Ltd.

Contents

The XB-70 is rolled out and revealed to the public for the first time. *AFMC/HO*

The authors would like to thank the individuals and organizations who supported us in the writing of this book over the past eight years. What follows is an extensive but almost certainly incomplete list of those who helped. We apologize to those we have left out; unfortunately our memories are no better than anyone else's. We would be glad to correct those omissions in any books we may be privileged to write and have published in the future.

We would like to offer special thanks to the following individuals for their outstanding "above and beyond the call of duty" assistance to us in the preparation of this book:

Dr. William Elliot, Air Force Materiel Command History Office, Wright-Patterson AFB; R. Eric Falk, General Electric Aircraft Engines; Charles R. Frey, USAF Museum; Mike Haenggi, Motorbooks International; Wesley B. Henry, USAF Museum; Lt. Col. Jack B. Hilliard, USAFR (Ret.), Former Curator, USAF Museum; Col. Joseph D. Hornsby, USAF (Ret.), Former Director, USAF Museum; MSgt. David Menard, USAF (Ret.), USAF Museum; Anthony Mazzone, Naval Inventory Control; Joe F. Skinner, USAF Museum (Ret.); Mary Anne Ruggiero, Phoenix Aviation Research; Robert Spaulding, USAF Museum; Walter Spivak (Chief designer XB-70, North American Aviation); Col. Richard L. Uppstrom, USAF (Ret.), Former Director, USAF Museum; Marti Ventolo, USAF Museum; John D. Weber, Command Historian, Air Force Materiel Command; Charles G. Worman, Curator, USAF Museum; John Whitenbury.

Our utmost appreciation and thanks also go to the following people who provided vital assistance to us:

Lt. Col. Nick Apple, USAF Museum (Ret.); Carol J. August, Air Force Materiel Command History Office; Diana Bachert, USAF Museum; Jim Benedict; Don Bergoson, B-70 Field Rep.,YJ-93 (Ret.) General Electric Aircraft Engines; Bobbie L. Bollinger, USAF Museum (Ret.); Sam Christian, Curator, Seabee Museum; Kari Clark, USAF Museum; Diana Cornelisse, Chief Historian, Aeronautical Systems Center History Office; Col. Joseph F. Cotton, USAF (Ret.); Mary Ann Cresswell, Department of Veterans' Affairs; Kirk Davenport, NASA SR-71 Ops, Edwards AFB; Pearlie Drayan, Air Force Association Photo Archives; William C. Fields, USAF Motion Picture Film Depository; Jeff Fisher, USAF Museum; Charles Gebhart, USAF Museum (Ret.); Joel & Susan Goldberg; Jan Goode; Glenn Hart, Intrepid Museum; James Hill, John F. Kennedy Library; Bonnie Holtmann, USAF Museum; Irvin Jobe, USAF Museum (Ret.); Dr. Dean Kallander, USAF Museum; Bob Koken, GE Aircraft Engines (Ret); John Kuntz, USAF Motion Picture Film Depository; Paul Lake, USAF Museum (Ret.); John Lample, British Airways; Master Vu and Master Eagle Graphic Services Inc.; Gloria & Jeff Brager; Mike Larson, Larson Color Labs; Mike Lichtman, Universal Photo Service; Jesse Lozano; John Lyons, USAF Museum (Ret.); Robert & Roberta May; Albert Misenko, Former Chief Historian, Aeronautical Systems Center (Ret.); Dan Oliver, USAF Museum; Gordon Pane, NASA SR-71 Ops., Edwards AFB; Vic Pendergast, GE Aircraft Engines (Ret); Ronald Petry, USAF Museum (Ret.); Domenic Proscia, Intrepid Museum; William R. Pyles, Enon Community Historical Society; Mike Relja, NASA SR-71 Ops., Edwards AFB; Joel M. Rose, Flagship Communications, Inc.; Rocky Rudaschel, North American / Rockwell, CA; Lee Saegaser, NASA History Office; Robert L. Shaw, Fighter Command International; Eric Simonsen, North American / Rockwell; Dan Stroud; George Torres, North American Aviation / Boeing Aircraft Corp; Denise Townsend, Boeing Aircraft Corp., HSCT Research; Gabriel F. Vacca, USAF Museum; Rita Westerfield, FAA Historical Records; Vivian White, USAF Museum (Ret.).

The following organizations are among those who provided outstanding support to us during the preparation of this book:

Air Force Materiel Command; Air Force Museum Foundation; Aeronautical Systems Center; Avco Corporation; Boeing Aircraft Company; Center for Air Force History; 88th Air Base Wing; Enon Community Historical Society; Fighter Command International; Flagship Communications, Inc.; General Electric Aircraft Engines; John F. Kennedy Library; Lockheed / Martin Advanced Development Projects (Skunkworks); Motorbooks International; NASA Photo Archives; North American Aviation, Inc.; Ohio History of Flight Museum; Phoenix Aviation Research; Rockwell International Corp.; Secretary of the Air Force Office of Public Affairs; U.S. Air Force Museum.

CHAPTER 1

The frontal view of Valkyrie was just as spectacular as any other. The world had never seen anything like it. She was unique in almost every way. *AFMC/HO*

An Introduction to Norse Mythology

THE NAME "VALKYRIE"

What does the name Valkyrie really mean? Valkyria (Valr: those slain in battle; and Kyria, related to the verb kiosa: to choose) means one who picks from among the war dead. In the Germanic translation, it refers to the daughters of Odin, the chief god of the Norsemen. They were the ones who rode to the battlefield and chose the dead warriors that they felt were worthy to serve Odin at Valhalla, the Hall of Valhol, or the Hall of the Slain. Valhalla supposedly had 540 doors, which could admit 800 of the slain warriors. The roof was made of battle shields. Valkyries were women warriors who would serve drinks of mead at the Hall of Valhol, and who could be just as comfortable riding into battle dressed in armor. They returned the "einherjar," or Odin's adopted sons, to him from the battlefield.

Some mythologists claim that there are only 9 Valkyries, while others claim there are 13—still others claim 25 or more. Some of their recorded names are Shaker, Mist, Axetime, Raging, Might, Shrieking, Host Fetter, Screaming, Spear Bearer, Shield Bearer, Wrecker of Plans, Kin of the Gods. To give you more background, and to show how the name fits into our story of the XB-70 "Valkyrie," you need to know a little bit of Norse mythology.

Asgard is the home of the gods. Unlike the heaven we envision, Asgard is a fearful place. There is no joy, although there is pleasure in serving Odin. That pleasure comes from the honor of fighting for him, and the fact that, before the warriors sat down to the great feast, all their wounds would be healed. Hanging over Asgard is the inescapable threat of doom. Even the gods cannot save themselves from the battle between good and evil. It is truly a hopeless situation, but they will fight to the end. They know that they cannot save themselves by any amount of courage or great deeds, but they do not give up, even in the face of overwhelming adversity. A brave death ensures a place in Valhalla. Death is not considered a loss. Rather, it is the conquering of evil by resisting the desire to yield to it—unto the end—even in the face of defeat.

Even though the Norse hero was lost if he didn't yield to the course of destruction, he could still choose between giving up and dying. He won Valhalla by continuing to fight and to resist evil even though it would avail him nothing but death.

The name "Valkyrie," picked by an Air Force sergeant so long ago, was really more than just a name that sounded good. It could never have been more appropriate. Not only was the Valkyrie a beautiful maiden who served as a warrior, she was the daughter of a god, and she stood for the finality of the battlefield. She was pleased to serve in the halls of Valhalla, dressed in the whitest of robes, or on the battlefield, clad in armor. Her weapons were lightning flashes, and the clouds were the divine steeds she rode over the rainbow known as "Bifrost" into battle, with dew dropping like diamonds from their manes.

That was the dream of the XB-70 Valkyrie program, to be the ultimate in the art of aerial warfare, the consummate weapons platform built for lethality and inherent grace and speed. But the Valkyrie was never given the chance. As with the ever present war between good and evil that went on outside of Valhalla, the B-70s program was constantly fought for—or against—on the floor of Congress, in the Oval Office, and in the Pentagon.

Just as in the myths, Valkyrie rose to the occasion and continued to give everything she had in the form of technological breakthroughs, such as honeycomb stainless steel and the new brazing technology that went with it; as well as the idea of boxing the six powerful YJ-93 engines together for the greatest in efficiency not only aerodynamically, but on the flight line, where an engine change could be done in about 25 minutes. These are concepts that continue to be used today. Even her flight deck

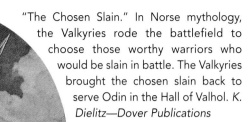

"The Chosen Slain." In Norse mythology, the Valkyries rode the battlefield to choose those worthy warriors who would be slain in battle. The Valkyries brought the chosen slain back to serve Odin in the Hall of Valhol. *K. Dielitz—Dover Publications*

arrangement has been explored by Boeing for the study of a new supersonic transport (SST) concept.

Like the heroes of the Norse myths, the XB-70 went on, even though her cause was futile. Through her efforts, and those of the people who sustained her, much of the technology that is used today is her gift. The politicians may have won the day—just as the fighting goes on outside of Valhalla, in the world of the Norsemen—but Valkyrie still returns to the battlefield, not in her true form, but in the heart of the technology and the people who built and flew her.

When you look at the Valkyrie as she is now, resting in the United States Air Force Museum, let your imagination run a little wild, and see her like the Norsemen did.

Valkyiur's Song
Slowly they moved to the billow side,
And the forms as they grew more clear,
Seemed each on a tall pale steed to ride,
And a shadowy crest to rear
And to beckon with faint hand
From the dark and rocky strand
And to point a gleaming spear,
There a stillness on his spirit fell,
Before an unearthly train;
For he knew Valhalla's daughters well,
"The Chooser of the Slain!"

Valkyrie's public debut captivated the imaginations of most of those who attended. She was an awesome sight, from her twin vertical stabilizers to her long, slender nose. *AFMC/HO*

A bright and sunny May 11, 1964, was the occasion for the XB-70 Valkyrie's rollout ceremony at North American Aviation's Palmdale, California, manufacturing facility. *Air Force Materiel Command Office of History, AFMC/HO*

CHAPTER 2

This artist's concept of the Valkyrie shows her speeding high over the earth. Note the vertical stabilizers are almost out of proportion with the rest of the aircraft. *AFMC/HO*

Waste of Technological Advantage

The XB-70 Valkyrie was one of the most remarkable aeronautical developments of the 1960s. It represented technology at its limits and rivaled the space program for the attention it garnered in the popular press. Although the Air Force had long anticipated a need for a triplesonic manned bomber as a replacement for its reliable Boeing B-52 Stratofortress, the XB-70 was never produced.

The reasons for not producing the bomber were mainly political, although projected high costs were partly responsible. The manned bomber was thought by missile advocates, Secretary of Defense Robert S. McNamara in particular, to have become outmoded. There were also conveniently cited studies that showed that the B-70 would be vulnerable to Soviet anti-aircraft missiles. Even so, a smaller, more stealthy, highly secret aircraft—with only somewhat better speed and altitude capability—was being developed by the Lockheed "Skunk Works." That aircraft later became known as the SR-71.

Political considerations that were first expressed in the second Eisenhower administration, and then later in the Kennedy administration, brought down the B-70 program. Opposition to the program in the early 1960s was personified, and reached beyond the program itself and out to its supporters. Distrust of the military advocates of the manned bomber combined with the belief in the efficiency of Intercontinental Ballistic Missiles (ICBMs) militated against the bomber's production. In the process, the technology developed for the B-70 was restricted to a research program that ended in 1969 with the retirement of XB-70 AV-1 (Air Vehicle #1).

The potential of the new aircraft was never realized and any potential for progress in developing a large Mach 3 aircraft, either military or civilian, was arrested. A serious consequence was a delay in the advancement of some of the related technology by as much as 20 years. There are people who point to the Concorde and conclude that it is an outgrowth of the XB-70, but that is not an accurate conclusion. The Concorde is a less advanced Mach 2 transport that has little in common with the XB-70.

The demise of the XB-70 and the B-70 program was but an example of a shortcoming in our political system when it attempts to influence practical scientific developments. Elected officials, most of whom have little knowledge or interest in things scientific, and appointed officials, who have their own political agendas, have demonstrated that they are ill-equipped to make the technological decisions required of them. The cost of the resulting waste is impossible to calculate.

EARLY CONCEPTS FOR A NEW BOMBER

The 1950s were a strange time for the United States. Not only was the country getting over the traumas of World War II and trying to instill in the American public a new sense of purpose, but it was also being confronted with the prospect of nuclear war. The Russian Bear loomed over Eastern Europe and it seemed as if nothing could stop its encroachment. The U.S. government was desperately trying to discover the Soviet Union's actual potential for unleashing nuclear devastation, while remaining placid in the eyes of the American public. A few things did leak out from behind the security shield; the so-called bomber gap and the missile gap being noteworthy and ultimately phony examples. The U.S. government's attempt to convey a peaceful attitude to the American public did not have the desired effect.

Back on October 14, 1954, General Curtis E. LeMay, then head of the Air Force's Strategic Air Command, wrote a secret letter to the Pentagon outlining what he thought should be the parameters for a new bomber to replace the B-52. LeMay wanted a bomber with a range of 6,000 miles without in-flight refueling, and he wanted a Mach 1+ cruising speed. His ambitions at the time, however, were restricted to a 600-mile-per-hour cruise and a supersonic dash capability of at least 1,000 miles per hour. Many felt that LeMay was being "rather determined" in his quest for the perfect weapons platform. After all, as he was so fond of saying, "Tomorrow's weapons must be designed yesterday."

Boeing and North American both entered the fray with competing proposals for the Air Force. They had been given just six months to come up with something to present. After the two companies submitted their initial designs, they found that they were remarkably similar. They were also so futuristic as to resemble something one might find in a science fiction or fantasy magazine. The two proposed bombers were also fantastic in projected weight: 1,000,000 pounds! This made it seem impossible to build the bomber of LeMay's dreams. The futuristic designs and massive projected weights raised an important fiscal and political question: Would the new bomber satisfy the Eisenhower camp in its quest for a tight budget?

EARLY OPPOSITION

There was opposition to the B-70 supersonic bomber program in the Eisenhower administration, well before John F. Kennedy took office. The Eisenhower administration had inherited the Korean War and along with it the Truman administration's apparent policy of surrendering to every military defense doomsayer who could gain a hearing within the establishment.

Truman's people had succumbed to the thinking that a defense buildup, spurred by the requirement for the United States to defend South Korea, would be able to pay for itself by the economic growth it would produce. Truman's administration had been very lax in the way it approved defense spending. It encouraged pumping money into the economy, but instead of bolstering growth, the money funded inflation and waste. Thus, upon taking office, the Eisenhower administration was left with a war to finish and a huge defense budget riddled with pork-barrel projects.

Eisenhower decided to change that. He believed that planning the defense of the nation was not a matter of funding for a single date in the future but instead a matter of establishing appropriate protection to be projected into the

President John F. Kennedy and Secretary of the Air Force Eugene M. Zuckert at Cape Canaveral in 1962. *John F. Kennedy Library*

future as the actions and apparent purposes of other countries around the world compelled. It was a policy that would have to be lived with over a period of years. Eisenhower intended to gain control of the defense budget and, throughout his eight years in office, sought to scale down the services.

Not surprisingly, Ike's attempts to carry out his policy changes were often hindered by misconceptions. In the 1950s many people believed that Dwight David Eisenhower was just a farm boy who had made the big time by becoming a World War II hero, thus propelling him toward the presidency. It was also widely believed at the time that Eisenhower wasn't exactly the intellectual that the presidency should attract. He wasn't comfortable with the social graces or the protocol needed to meet a head of state or a big-time industrialist. Well, that was what some people thought. Eisenhower, however, was actually a very powerful, effective president, but that fact wasn't brought out until much later, years after his death. He did have a vision for the United States, and that vision didn't always include what the military wanted in the way of new weapons systems.

There was to be more reliance on the nuclear option than on conventional warfare. Eisenhower decided that he did not want any more limited wars. His administration was abandoning the idea that any future war could be fought without recourse to nuclear weapons. To his critics, Eisenhower was quick to defend the legitimate use of nuclear weapons and his determination to use them, if necessary. He said that, ". . . because America's most precious possession is the lives of her citizens, we should base our security upon military formations which make maximum use of science and technology. . . ."

Since the United States would rely on its nuclear strike capability, the only available delivery system was the manned bomber fleet, and the Air Force managed to hold out against many of the budget cuts. The Army and the Navy did not fare as well. While there was a place for manned bombers in delivering nuclear weapons, the newly developing Intercontinental Ballistic Missile (ICBM) promised a more economical defense. One might have thought that as long as there still had to be manned bombers, a new more capable bomber would have been acceptable to the administration, even under a policy of significant cutbacks. On the other hand, in the early-to-mid-1950s, the Air Force had the B-36 intercontinental bomber, the B-47 medium bomber, and coming on in the middle part of the decade would be the B-52 Stratofortress. With the addition of the B-58 supersonic bomber by the end of the decade, many believed there was no urgency in developing yet another bombing platform, no matter how much more capability it might provide.

So, the B-70 was to have been the very-high-altitude, triplesonic replacement for the B-52. The B-52 was just entering the Air Force inventory in the mid-1950s. Before

A photo taken at General Electric's Large Jet Engine facility at Cincinnati, Ohio, on October 11, 1962. Shown are Mr. B. W. Bruckmann, J93 engine project manager (extreme left); Maj. Fitzhugh Fulton (standing center); Lt. Col. Joe Cotton (seated center); Mr. Al White (center foreground), with Mr. O. E. Deal, North American Aviation (near right); and Col. Guy Townsend, XB-70 joint test force director (far right). The occasion was an orientation course given by General Electric that included test cell throttle operation at a simulated speed of 2,000 miles per hour in General Electric's Ram Test facility. *GE Aircraft Engines via R. Eric Falk*

the end of the decade, the planning for the new bomber, known originally as WS-110A or Weapon System 110A, was well underway and the design of the airframe had been pretty well established.

Even though it began to receive project funding in the late 1950s, the B-70 bomber was seen by financial planners as much too expensive to satisfy the administration's desire to maintain a thrifty economic policy, and in late 1959 the development program was canceled. This despite the president's declaration that the maximum use of science and technology could substitute for larger military forces.

A full-scale mockup had even been approved in 1959. By 1960, *Aviation Week* was publishing photos of a model that represented a more or less final configuration. It was an on-again, off-again affair, but the fact is that the program was canceled well before the first flight of the number one airplane. The reasons for the cancellation were political as well as budgetary. When the final word came, it broke the hearts of thousands of people who worked on

President John F. Kennedy and former President Dwight D. Eisenhower with military advisor on April 22, 1961. *John F. Kennedy Library*

Swearing-in ceremony for Secretary of the Air Force Eugene Zuckert, January 23, 1961. Left to right: Mrs. Kennedy, Mrs. Lyman Lemnitzer, President Kennedy, Secretary Zuckert, and Frederick Korth. *John F. Kennedy Library*

Valkyrie. By that time, over $300 million had been spent on the B-70's development.

The U.S. Air Force wanted, and needed, an intercontinental bomber, and it fought the administration to have the canceled funding restored. The Air Force's campaign was brought to the Congress and handled on the floor of the Senate by Senator Carl Vinson (D) GA, chairman of the Senate Armed Services Committee. There was quite a good fight played out in both houses of Congress. Pentagon and congressional protests against the cancella-

tion were so strong that by the mid-1950s, advisors to President Eisenhower recommended that the program be continued with minimum funding. It was largely a political move because in the run-up to the November elections, the Republicans were being hammered by the Democrats on defense issues. There was still the question of a bomber gap between the United States and the Soviet Union, and until Kelly Johnson and his U-2 creation proved that the "gap" theory was invalid, the option of attempting to narrow the gap with more U.S. bombers had to be protected.

In July 1960, Congress approved $75 million in additional funding for the B-70, which brought its fiscal year 1961 total to $365 million. Later, Congress recommended that the $75 million be raised to $190 million, but without any assurance that the administration would actually spend the money. Three months after the Kennedy administration took office, the new secretary of defense, Robert McNamara, canceled the production program and authorized the construction of only three experimental research aircraft. In July 1961, the $365 million previously approved by Congress for Fiscal Year 1961 was reduced to $75 million. Although the plan called for 250 B-70s to be delivered starting in 1962, the program was cut back to 13, and then to just 3 research vehicles.

MCNAMARA'S FOLLY

Along with the establishment of the new Kennedy administration came new players in the game of "B-70," and Secretary McNamara and General Curtis LeMay, who had commanded the 305th Bomb Group, the 3rd Air Division, and ultimately the XX Bomber Command in World War II, were prime players among them. LeMay knew the value of being able to depend on a bomber force. As noted earlier, he had headed up the Strategic Air Command, then became vice chief of staff of the Air Force in the Eisenhower administration. President Kennedy would later appoint him chief of staff of the Air Force.

Robert McNamara was known to have no great fondness for the military in general and the Air Force in particular. McNamara had served under General Curtis LeMay during World War II as a statistical control officer and was not especially fond of him. He frowned upon some of LeMay's statistical accounting methods. Later on, he easily found fault with the weapons systems favored by his former boss.

McNamara was not enamored of the B-70 program that LeMay supported. He felt that too much money was being spent on such weapons systems and preferred the neatness and economy of the ICBM and the theory of Mutually Assured Destruction. Not surprisingly, LeMay was an advocate of strategic bombing and all of its components, and was not in favor of putting all of his strategic eggs in one basket, namely a fleet of ICBMs.

There was the familiar argument in favor of the

Secretary of Defense Robert S. McNamara and President John F. Kennedy in the White House, June, 1962. *John F. Kennedy Library*

ICBMs: "Why would we need bombers when ICBMs can do the same job cheaper, more reliably, and without endangering bomber crews?" It was a good question and there was no disputing those qualities of the ICBM. But there also were the familiar counterarguments: "You can't recall an ICBM once it's launched so, as a bargaining chip in a crisis, the ICBM is an all-or-nothing proposition." Bombers can be launched, used as threats, feints, and decoys, and recalled in the nick of time, if necessary. Bombers didn't have to be hidden away in so-called hardened silos. If the international situation went sour, they would already be in the air by the time enemy missiles arrived. Besides, how do you do bomb damage assessment with an ICBM? Bombers were seen as our second strike capability. Whatever side you take, it's clear that ICBMs and bombers carry out different kinds of strikes. Each has its strengths and weaknesses.

The stir raised in the Kennedy administration over the role and expertise of the military made earlier arguments over the XB-70 and other contemporary programs pale by comparison. McNamara intended to completely revamp the Department of Defense, perhaps even to the extent of doing away with the individual service secretaries and, by implication, the individual military services themselves. It was not a new idea, but it certainly put the services on the defensive.

McNamara had the confidence of President Kennedy and had the president's authority to assert more rigid civilian control over the military establishment. Before agreeing to take the job of secretary of defense, he asked for and received assurance from Kennedy that he would have complete control of the Department of Defense, subject only to the higher authority of the president as commander in chief.

McNamara assembled in the DOD a group of intellectual "Whiz Kids" to propagate new theories as to the proper place of the military in the Kennedy administration. The military establishment saw many of the so-called Whiz Kids as arrogant and inexperienced. In many instances these newcomers left no doubt that they held the military leadership in outright contempt. For his part, McNamara would listen to the representations of the military leadership but did not hesitate to discount the advice he received. His perception of the military chiefs, too, at times seemed to be characterized by a not-so-vague contempt for their expertise, as well as for that of the military establishment as a whole. In turn, McNamara and his people were perceived by their critics as "eggheads," whose intellectual viewpoints often clashed with practical realities. Kennedy, on the other hand, though an intellectual and a politician, was more practical and would override his defense chief when necessary. It didn't happen often, though, because the two men were closely allied in their thinking.

As indicated earlier, LeMay was a staunch supporter of the XB-70 as the next logical step in the modernization of the Air Force's bomber fleet. To say that he did not see eye-to-eye with Secretary McNamara would be an understatement. General LeMay described Secretary McNamara as having a "bombastic confidence" in the ability of the United States to retaliate effectively with ICBMs. McNamara was noted for his reliance on statistics and little else. If there existed a concept, or even a piece of hardware, that he could not reduce to numbers or a chart, there was a good chance that he would question its value. The B-70 was a complex aircraft and the program for its development was likewise complex and expensive.

True to form, McNamara disliked the program for the very reason that its complexities could not easily be reduced to figures on a flip chart. Despite his later claims to the contrary, there is solid evidence that he would not accept any testimony about the airplane's potential as a long-range bomber. He even claimed that the B-70 could not be used to drop conventional bombs but could only launch short-range attack or cruise missiles. This supposed lack of conventional bombing potential of the aircraft was used as one of his reasons to discredit the B-70 program. Yet McNamara wanted to have the Air Force put the bombers on 24-hour alert, even to the extent of having some of them actually in the air 24 hours a day, just in case there would be an enemy strike that would put the bombers in jeopardy. So much for his faith in NORAD, Cheyenne Mountain, and SAC.

One must consider that in the early 1960s, after the new Kennedy Administration took office and Robert McNamara became secretary of defense, new decisions were coming due on such programs as the B-70. Under McNamara, the DOD civilian leadership had already con-

17

Swearing in of White House staff, 1961. *John F. Kennedy Library*

cluded that the military leadership did not know what it was doing. In one sense McNamara's civilians were correct. Even in the military there is not necessarily a consensus. There are many different factions pulling against one another, and this was certainly the case during the development of the B-70. Not only was there interservice rivalry among the military branches, there was rivalry within the Air Force—among the bomber supporters, the ICBM proponents, the interceptor aficionados, the reconnaissance, intelligence, and other communities. For these groups the game was to try to get the most money for your favorite program.

NASA was a heavy player in the budget wars, too. While NASA drew on Air Force manpower and other resources to get the space program underway, it was busy trying to cut itself away from reliance on the military for space program support. It did not succeed, but for a time NASA tried mightily. In any event, the McNamara philosophy was carried on into the Johnson administration with the full support of President Johnson himself.

Another factor that led to the demise of the B-70 program was, for lack of a better word, inattention. Somehow, it seemed that DOD leadership, the Congress, the administration—and even some Air Force leaders—had lost track of what the B-70 was supposed to accomplish. Their focus had simply slipped. The leadership quit looking at what was to have been a high-speed, manned, intercontinental bomber. Instead, they saw the aircraft only in the narrow context of a purely experimental program that they thought would have no immediate military application. That kind of tunnel vision was going on at the same time the super-secret A-12 was being considered for an attack role using short-range attack missiles or longer range cruise missiles. It was the same role McNamara had already rejected for the B-70. According to McNamara, the cost of the proposed fleet of B-70s would have totaled somewhere around $20 billion over 10 years. This would have been much more than the cost of the Minuteman ICBM program. At the same time, however, the CIA was busy promoting the A-12 to President Kennedy as an interceptor. It was, once again, not what you knew, but whose ear you had in the White House.

The argument over whether the support for the B-70 should be withdrawn or bolstered ranged over two years. There was the infamous deal between Senator Carl Vinson, then head of the House Armed Services Committee (and a B-70 supporter), and President Kennedy, made in the White House Rose Garden. McNamara had refused to spend funds assigned to the B-70 program by using an obscure power created in a 1958 change in the National Security Act. So much was Kennedy enamored of his secretary of defense that he worked out a deal with Vinson so that Congress would let McNamara have his way. It was known that McNamara did not have the political savvy to work out a situation in the normal Washington style, so the president, using his political skills with Vinson, had helped.

McNamara reacted to events like an on-off switch. It was all or nothing. That kind of attitude didn't cut it with Congress, the epitome of compromise. Figures didn't lie, McNamara believed; but he also knew that figures could be manipulated to prove anything. He had, at least, learned the basics.

THE TFX

There was another factor guiding Robert McNamara. In the 1960s, defense contractors were also competing for an aircraft contract under the TFX (Tactical Fighter "X"), or F-111 program. This was a joint Navy and Air Force program to develop a fighter that could be used by both services, ostensibly to preserve the idea of economy through commonality between them. The fact that the Navy really didn't want the TFX made no difference. In November 1962, the Department of Defense (i.e., McNamara) decided the TFX would be produced by General Dynamics, Fort Worth. Texas, of course, was—not so coincidentally—the home state of Vice President Lyndon Johnson. The go-ahead for the F-111 program, and selection of General Dynamics as the contractor, would be a political plus for the Kennedy administration, and would be the ideal payback to the vice president for his ultimate support of Kennedy's election to the presidency. The selection of General Dynamics of Fort Worth as the TFX prime contractor was announced at a rally and a breakfast that was given at the Texas Hotel, the morning of the day that Kennedy would be assassinated in Dallas.

The money for the F-111 had to come from somewhere, and what better place to begin looking for it than to cut a program the administration did not like in the first place? So McNamara cut the B-70 bomber program back to three experimental research XB-70s and laid down the law governing budgets and bombers. He would have his way with the military and his way, he believed, would

Gen. Taylor, President Kennedy, and Secretary McNamara at the White House, January 25, 1963. *John F. Kennedy Library*

dissuade any aggressor from mounting a first strike against the United States. The only problem was that the dissuasion theory was not foolproof. One could not recall an ICBM; that is, one could not threaten to carry out a strike, then withdraw the threat as a diplomatic strategy. Once an ICBM was launched there was no turning back.

In the context of ICBM-only operations, the MAD (Mutually Assured Destruction) theory was appalling in concept. Simply put, a defender guarantees nuclear destruction to its attacker by making it impossible to destroy all the defender's warheads in a preemptive strike. If an

19

Artist's concept of XB-70. Note the rounded leading and trailing edges of the canards, the blunted nose and the lack of fold-down wing tips. *AFMC/HO*

attacker flattens the defending country with a nuclear strike, it will soon suffer the same fate and become the recipient of a large reserve of the defender's missiles launched from hardened silos and submarines. If you destroy us, we will destroy you. Even the dropping of the A-bombs on Japan could not really be compared with the cynicism implied by the MAD theory. At least there was a large body of thought that agreed that use of the A-bombs was necessary in bringing an end to a brutal war. Millions of lives may very well have been saved by ending the war there and then. Two bombs were dropped and that was it. With ICBMs only, MAD simply ended everything for everyone, with little chance left to go back and rebuild.

Much of the MAD theory was supported by the Air Force brass. It was one of General LeMay's selling points and he had built the Strategic Air Command upon it to

some extent. But he also had the bomber fleet, and the presence of that fleet provided for the possibility of something less than total destruction.

ZUCKERT VS. MCNAMARA VS. LEMAY

When President Kennedy came to office in 1961, he appointed Eugene Zuckert as secretary of the Air Force and, in what some people saw as a surprise move, appointed General Curtis E. LeMay as chief of staff of the Air Force. Even during his first year in office, Zuckert became disenchanted with what he perceived as a usurpation of his power by Secretary McNamara.

McNamara was working the Reorganization Act of 1958 to his full benefit. He was also imposing himself over many of the service secretaries. Eugene Zuckert was so troubled by McNamara that he thought about resigning. Nonetheless, Zuckert decided to fight back and redefine his role as the Air Force secretary. He stayed on in an attempt to restore the authority of his office, and to try to help the Air Force reacclimate itself to McNamara and his Whiz Kids. Zuckert knew McNamara, having met him in 1940 at Harvard Business School. Zuckert even recommended McNamara for appointment as assistant secretary of the Air Force for management in 1962.

McNamara's way of doing business was to reduce things to his level. Everything was going to be brought to the level of numbers and statistics. Using his ability to analyze anything to its death, McNamara wanted to remove the emotional side of making decisions about military hardware. In this case, "emotional decisions" could only have referred to the innate ability of military chiefs to make decisions on questions that directly concerned their particular service.

McNamara wanted Zuckert to fall into line with his new policy of rational, detailed decision making and also accept his ever present suggestions. McNamara wanted everything centralized as far as the Pentagon went and would accept no less from any service, particularly the Air Force.

Zuckert felt the strain of working with McNamara and his incessant demand for information for just about everything; so much so, that Zuckert would complain about not having enough time to do his work because of all the meetings and other demands levied upon him. He couldn't concentrate on other issues such as arms control that he believed merited his attention.

So Zuckert teamed up with General LeMay. Due to the Reorganization Act of 1958, many of the available roads to the chain of command had been closed to the service secretaries. LeMay, knowing of the situation and aware of the value of his access to the Joint Chiefs of Staff, promised to keep an eye on things for Zuckert. He would let Zuckert know if issues arose where pressure needed to be applied to influence the adoption of desirable policies that might otherwise have been rejected.

It was well known that large segments of the military staff were intensely contemptuous of McNamara's Whiz Kids. Zuckert felt that many of the McNamara staff had little or no experience in advising and making policy for military professionals who had far more experience than the Whiz Kids could ever hope for. This meant that while the Whiz Kids may have been capable of trying to figure out strategic weapons theory, they didn't have a clue about how to utilize men, materiel, and aircraft. This was causing much consternation among the military professionals.

General LeMay was one of the first to proclaim that McNamara and his staff were not listening to the leaders of the military services. He felt that they really had not the faintest idea of how to deal with the threat of communism. He thought their theory of trying to counter a hostile nation on a weapon-for-weapon basis instead of using superlative force and strategy against it was not only senseless, but potentially deadly to this country. This didn't affect McNamara and his quest for centralization. He was determined to take authority away from the service secretaries and the military chiefs.

Zuckert was getting more and more frustrated with the budget cutting and loss of tactical power in his position. McNamara was unrelenting in his quest for the perfect budget and many of the service secretaries and assistant secretaries were at their wits' end, including General LeMay. LeMay was finding out that he was being short-changed on many of his requests in the Air Force budget. He was short-changed when some of the already-planned-for B-52s were deleted, he was short-changed when it came to the B-70 funding, and he was short-changed even when it came to getting more Minuteman missiles.

Zuckert was trying to fight back by cutting around some of the policies being laid down by McNamara, but it was becoming increasingly difficult to avoid them. A lot of information was not getting passed down the chain of command from the Department of Defense. Zuckert was finding that he was not being included in many meetings that the Department of Defense was having with NASA concerning missile test range operations. After much arguing, the Air Force was finally included but not before Zuckert had to go to bat and state that the so-called "spirit of cooperation" between the Air Force and the office of the director of research and engineering under Harold Brown was definitely in jeopardy of being colored in a repulsive and unprofessional way.

This leads to a very interesting point. At this time in 1961, McNamara was already proposing that all public relations functions be directed through the office of the secretary of defense. It was known that McNamara didn't like the idea that there was so much publicity about the space program and the Air Force in the press. He also made sure that NASA was thrown into the issue; he controlled its publicity output so that it also coincided with the controlled Air Force output. Zuckert made sure that even though the Air Force had to run all its public relations functions through the Office of the Secretary of Defense, it at least maintained some control over them. In March of 1961, Zuckert created a new office called the Special Assistant for Public Affairs just for that purpose.

Zuckert's trials in the public relations arena were not over, though. A new office was created for the secretary of defense as well—the Office of the Assistant Secretary of Defense for Public Affairs. This office was run by Arthur Sylvester, whose duty it was to withhold any information he felt was sensitive. For example, this meant that he withheld dates and locations of missile test firings to prevent the acquisition of "developmental chronologies." He controlled the photographing of weapons and facilities. Apparently, he even believed it was necessary to "protect"

An artist's concept of XB-70, which shows vortices forming on the canards and vertical stabilizers as she flies high above the earth.

certain areas of the space program as well.

Vendors to the government were becoming anxious and overwrought with the effort of trying to get their press releases, brochures, photos, films, and the like through the Department of Defense clearance process. Sylvester was to blame, and McNamara was definitely becoming an embarrassment in the public relations realm. Everything had to be cleared. It was a long drawn-out battle just to get the simplest information out and it seems that in 1961 it came to a head. McNamara and Sylvester had already taken over the press briefings, and were making statements before the services even knew anything about the subject of the briefings. Zuckert was—and had to be—on guard for the Air Force. He effectively went to bat to protect the Air Force because information pertaining to the Air Force was not being represented correctly. And as always, Zuckert also stood for the rest of the service secretaries. It was because of Zuckert's efforts that the newly formed Defense

Intelligence Agency (DIA), created by McNamara, was kept from consolidating all of the services' intelligence activities under one umbrella.

By and large Zuckert was supportive of General LeMay and the other Pentagon Air Force generals, and often served as a middle-man in attempts to get their views a fair hearing within the Administration. Throughout his tenure he also was a supporter of the B-70 program and the XB-70, but after leaving office Zuckert had a change of heart because he thought the cost of the Valkyrie was too high and her effectiveness would have been questionable had she been fielded. Then, too, there was an Administration and a Congress, each with its own budget priorities. The Congress was, in general, supportive of the B-70 program and was politically attempting to coerce the Kennedy Administration into continuing it. On the other hand, Kennedy and McNamara were opposed to spending more money on a bomber they agreed they didn't want, especially if it was at the cost of their darling TFX project.

Ultimately, President Kennedy made that noteworthy deal with House Armed Services Committee Chairman Carl Vinson—the one-time strong supporter of the B-70 program and the XB-70—and eventually funds over and above a two-airplane research project were dried up. Apparently, Vinson was convinced that another Congressional battle over funding the bomber would be too politically costly to pursue.

THE VIETNAM WAR

With the assassination of President Kennedy on November 22, 1963, and the succession of Lyndon B. Johnson to the presidency, a new set of factors was fed into the national defense equation. Probably nothing had more impact on the decisions of the civilian leadership concerning the XB-70 than did the distractions of the Vietnam War. The conflict had escalated following the Gulf of Tonkin incident, and Johnson and McNamara began to exert more heavily their influence over the military services charged with carrying out national policy.

As the Vietnam War became an ever important issue, Johnson's personality and McNamara's philosophy led to the running of the most minute operations of the war from the situation room of the White House. While military people on site and in Washington gave their advice time and time again, they found themselves ignored or overruled by the civilian leadership. Instead, in much the same way as Adolph Hitler (an admittedly extreme but perhaps apt example) had often overruled his military leaders during World War II, the civilian leaders in Washington felt they knew best how to handle the military situation. They actually ordered air strikes—or canceled or forbade air strikes—without the benefit of sound military judgment.

There may have been some unknown reasoning behind this state of affairs. The Vietnam War was a very political undertaking, and military leaders are by law, regulation, tradition, and Constitution, forbidden to get involved in politics. Perhaps some of the civilian political leaders believed their involvement was necessary so that the military would not have to make awkward political decisions for which they were neither trained nor entitled to make.

Whatever the precise truth of the matter, it was this mode of operation that carried on into subsequent administrations and led to the defeat of U.S. forces in Southeast Asia. The military experts, who had always acknowledged their subservience to civilian authority, could not do what they had been "hired" to do. This concept was already in place and being carried out on many of the defense programs including the B-70 program. Their military expertise had been discounted and undermined by the arrogance of the civilian authority. It was the same civilian authority that had decreed the "body count" mentality, and in some cases selected the more compliant of their military favorites to run the war as dictated from Washington. It was an

unprecedented situation. It was the first time in American history that the U.S. military establishment had been given a job and then had been expressly denied the authority to carry it out. No wonder that so many military professionals were disillusioned.

So, following the established pattern, programs such as the B-70, Skybolt, DynaSoar, and others supported by the various factions in the military—and particularly the Air Force—were given little support. The reluctance of the civilian leadership to support such programs existed because they had, within their own echelons, deliberately created a climate of mistrust for the military. Having spent a great deal of effort in creating that climate, this elite leadership simply could not bear to support the stated requirements of the services they claimed were untrustworthy. That would mean abandoning their foregone conclusions and returning a small amount of the power and prerogatives that they had so studiously usurped in the first place.

THE ROLE OF TECHNOLOGY

We don't know just how well Robert McNamara really understood new technology. He was a numbers man. Given the state of the new Kennedy administration, and a United States that was tired of the Cold War and fearful of the USSR, the road seemed clear to the White House and the secretary of defense. It also proved just how shortsighted Robert McNamara could be.

Between McNamara and John Kennedy, the two managed to build up the nuclear arms threat to mammoth proportions. They used the "might makes fright" theory to alarm the Soviet Union as well as the American public, regardless of the fact that aerial reconnaissance information was showing the White House that the Soviets had nowhere near the strength in their missile reserves that had originally been estimated. There was still an imbalance in strategic arms, but in favor of the United States, not the Soviet Union. In a sudden reversal, the U.S. "missile gap" quietly turned into to a U.S. "missile overload."

The new secretary of defense was using his old boardroom tactic of "any decision was better than no decision." Ben Rich commented in his book, *Skunk Works*, that when he and Kelly Johnson went to see Robert McNamara to sell the idea of an A-12 interceptor (the YF-12), Mr. McNamara was having lunch and reading some kind of report. So, the detailed presentation that Johnson and Rich had prepared was largely ignored. McNamara did not even look up at them until they were finished, even though there were charts aplenty. Apparently, McNamara was not going to allow himself to be swayed in any direction. Ben Rich later teased Kelly Johnson with the comment that "you shouldn't try to pitch anyone who was reading and eating until they were finished." It was an "interesting" way to treat two professionals of the caliber of Ben Rich and Kelly

This artist's idea conceptualized the B-70 with high, wide delta-shaped canards, shorter fold-down wing tips and beveled delta leading edges. *AFMC/HO*

President Kennedy and retiring Air Force Chief of Staff Gen. Thomas D. White, June 1961. *USAF Museum*

Johnson, but that was the way that Robert McNamara treated many people in the military and aerospace world—with contempt. Perhaps it never dawned on Mr. McNamara that he could be wrong about anything.

McNamara was determined to keep the B-70 bomber program limited to two experimental XB-70 aircraft prototypes, even with the foreknowledge that a third planned air vehicle was to be drastically different. He had to have known, too, that NASA had already committed to a contract to place SST research equipment in AV-2—thus making it feasible and cost-effective to continue.

Gen. Curtis E. LeMay and President Kennedy at LeMay's swearing in as chief of staff of the Air Force, June 30, 1961. *USAF Museum*

President Kennedy touring Cape Canaveral, 1962. *USAF Museum*

CHAPTER 3

XB-70 Valkyrie in flight formation with B-58 Hustler. *Photo courtesy AFMC/HO*

B-70 Development

COLD WAR REQUIREMENTS

The B-70 development program has a tangled history. The idea for the airplane that eventually became the XB-70 was actually conceived in the early 1950s during the buildup of the Cold War. It was to have been the very-high-altitude, triplesonic replacement for the B-52. The B-52 was just entering the Air Force inventory in the mid-1950s. The planning for the new bomber, known originally as WS-110A or Weapon System 110A, was well underway before the end of the 1950s and the design of the airframe had been pretty well established. A full-scale mockup had even been approved in 1959. By 1960, *Aviation Week* magazine was publishing photos of a model that represented a more or less final configuration.

Both Boeing and Convair began a study for the possibilities of a supersonic bomber in 1948. The Air Force's project enabled them to examine the credibility of a bomber capable of short supersonic dashes in combat. After a year and a half, following tests and looking at the canceled XB-55 program, they determined that they could meet the parameters for this supersonic bomber. As early as February 1951, and on into August 1952, the aircraft began to take shape. The idea gelled and became a bomber reconnaissance aircraft with medium- to long-range capability, maximum speeds of Mach 1.6 to 1.8, and in-flight refueling by aerial tankers.

At the time, there was hope that the J-47-X24 engine could be used for both Boeing's and Convair's designs. This engine was the precursor of the J-79, and it could meet all the requirements for the new weapons that were coming on line. The Wright Air Development Center (WADC) noted that there were unique differences between the designs of the two companies. WADC recommended elimination of Boeing from the program because it felt that Convair had a better handle on the planning goals, and suggested that Boeing should be studying a thermonuclear delivery system, a new propulsion system, zip fuels, and other developments. Convair was awarded the project under Air Force contract number AF33(038)-21250, which ran from February 1951 to August 1952 and which eventually became the B-58 Hustler.

The Strategic Air Command (SAC), on the other hand, supported Boeing with a letter dated March 30, 1952, to the director of requirements at Air Force Headquarters stating that Boeing and the Air Force had a commitment to the B-52 production program and that the "Air Force should reaffirm its operational requirements for a long-range bomber capable of delivering the most destructive warheads available from bases on this continent." SAC believed that manned flight at high altitudes and long ranges were an all-time priority for the Air Force development program. It also claimed that the Air Force,

View of the electrical fuse panel in the equipment bay of XB-70 Valkyrie AV-1 on display at the USAF Museum. *Authors*

having already developed the H-bomb and parasiting techniques, had demonstrated a continuing need for a program to develop long-range, heavy-payload bombers.

The letter also referred to studies that would eventually lead to the design and production of the ultimate in heavy bombers: one that would carry an H-bomb from the United States to a target destination and return to its base. The bomber should incorporate the longest range, highest altitude, and fastest speed, and meet all the requirements for military payloads and defensive systems. As a result of this letter, Boeing got the AF33(616)-2070 contract, which provided for a one-year design study for an advanced strategic weapons system. The study was to begin on May 1, 1953.

Boeing had pegged the time frame of operational status at 1960-1965 because of the size of the weapons involved. At the time, Boeing thought that it would be difficult to develop a weapon system capable of delivering thermonuclear weapons at intercontinental ranges. By May 1954, there was some improvement in reducing the size of these weapons so that they could be carried by conventional aircraft. That aided the motivation in developing

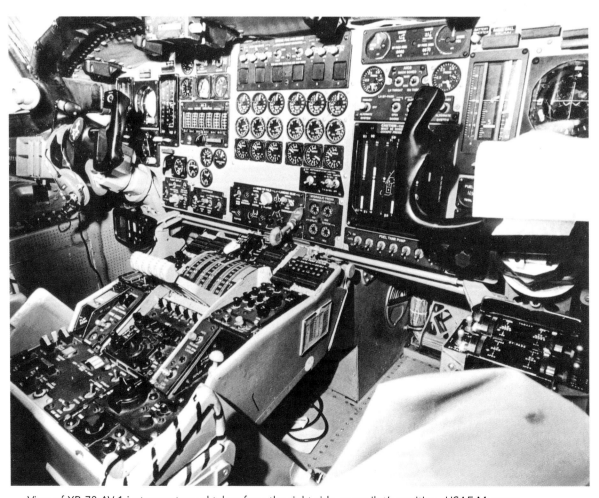

View of XB-70 AV-1 instrument panel taken from the right side or copilot's position. *USAF Museum*

This view of the center section of the instrument panel of the XB-70 #20001 highlights the throttles and engine instruments. *Authors*

an advanced aircraft. The design study to determine the new aircraft's design was known as MX-2145.

Thus, the development of the XB-70 as we know it began early in 1954 with Boeing Aircraft Corporation's MX-2145 project to study the type of weapon system required to deliver nuclear weapons. Among the systems investigated were manned and unmanned long-range conventional bombers as well as a proposal for a bomber powered by nuclear engines. The Air Force also received similar bomber proposals from Convair and Lockheed.

In the fall of 1954, the Air Force issued General Operational Requirement No. 38 (GOR 38) for a piloted, long-range bomber to replace the B-52 beginning in 1965. It was envisioned to be a conventionally powered, subsonic aircraft. In March 1955, the Air Force issued GOR 82, which superseded GOR 38. GOR 82 was not very much more detailed, but did specify that the bomber was to be capable of delivering up to 25,000 pounds of nuclear weapons. The new bomber was to have intercontinental range, like the B-52 it would replace.

Development of the aircraft and systems would be directed by the Air Research and Development Command (ARDC). ARDC issued Study Requirement No. 22 (SR 22), which gave the aircraft a developmental identity: Weapon System 110A. ARDC's study requirement also

was more specific about the bomber's desired capabilities. It was to have a minimum cruise speed of Mach 0.9 and a supersonic dash capability.

Early in 1955 the Air Force issued GOR 96, which added a reconnaissance version of the bomber to previous requirements. This version was to be known as WS 110L and, when combined with WS 110A, the designation WS 110A/L was applied. In mid-1955 the Air Staff ordered that WS 110A/L enter development competition as soon as possible. Several potential contractors were notified of the upcoming competition, but the only proposals were submitted by Boeing and North American Aviation.

Initially, the Air Force awarded letter contracts to both Boeing and North American in November 1955 for Phase I of WS 110A/L development. Definitive contracts followed in 1956. The contractors were required to provide a design, models, drawings, specifications, and a mockup of their proposed aircraft. The Air Force wanted to be able to inspect the mockup within two years.

WS 110A/L was to be an all-weather bomber that could operate day or night with an unrefueled range of 4,000 nautical miles. It was to have the additional capability of being aerial-refueled to extend its range to 5,500 nautical miles, or more if possible. The carriage of nuclear

This view from the cockpit of XB-70 AV-1 looking aft shows the head of the third fuel tank and, just forward of it, the large cooling water flash tanks. *Authors*

weapons remained a primary requirement. In addition to the minimum cruise speed of Mach 0.9, and supersonic dash capability, the aircraft was to be able to maintain an altitude of 60,000 feet over the target.

The Air Force judged the original design proposals submitted by North American and Boeing in 1956 to be unsatisfactory. The original designs were much too heavy, and the provisions for carrying fuel were too cumbersome. One idea envisioned huge floating outer wing panels and fuel tanks attached to a central fuselage. General Curtis LeMay likened the design to "three fuel tanks flying in formation." Since the Air Force clearly saw these early designs as impractical, Boeing and North American were sent back to the drawing boards to come up with something more reasonable.

A beautiful wide detail cockpit photo of XB-70 AV-1 instrument panel and center console layout. *Jim Benedict*

This photo provides a good look at the arrangement of the XB-70's windshield and nose ramp arrangement. Its two positions are illustrated in the diagram on page 32. *AFMC/HO*

In 1957, the Air Force redefined its requirements for the bomber and issued them to Boeing and North American. The Air Force now required an all-supersonic cruise—Mach 3.0 plus—capability instead of the subsonic-cruise/supersonic-dash capability that it had asked for previously. Altitude was increased from 60,000, to 70,000, to 75,000 feet, and range was increased from 5,500, to 6,000, to more than 10,000 miles. The gross weight of the aircraft would now be just under 500,000 pounds. The two competitors responded with their proposals, and by the end of the year, the Air Force evaluators briefed their findings to the Air Force Council. At the end of December 1957, the Air Force announced the selection of North American Aviation as the winner of the B-70 competition. The B-70 would be expensive, but the Air Force had established a requirement for a bomber that could deliver nuclear weapons to the Soviet Union and fly so fast and so high that no defense systems, whether they were fighters or surface-to-air missiles, could ever knock it down. The Air Force wanted to buy up to 250 such bombers.

COMPRESSION LIFT AND THE CUTTING EDGE

The exploration of Mach-speed flight began with Chuck Yeager's October 14, 1947, flight of the Bell XS-1 (later called the X-1). The XS-1, with its simple .45 caliber bullet-shaped airframe powered by a rocket engine, was dropped from a B-29 mother ship and broke the speed of sound. From that point on, something changed drastically in aviation every day. Higher and faster was the norm. Soon, the X-15 explored the hypersonic realm, and the B-58 Hustler delved into the region of routine supersonic flight of larger aircraft. The XB-70 Valkyrie was in the middle of it all, and she would be the fastest, highest flying, and largest supersonic aircraft ever. The XB-70 was one of the most complex aircraft ever built, especially when one considers the fact that most of the development was done as the building took place. Innovations abounded, and so did problems. The XB-70 entered a realm that aeronautics had not yet breached: sustained supersonic cruise.

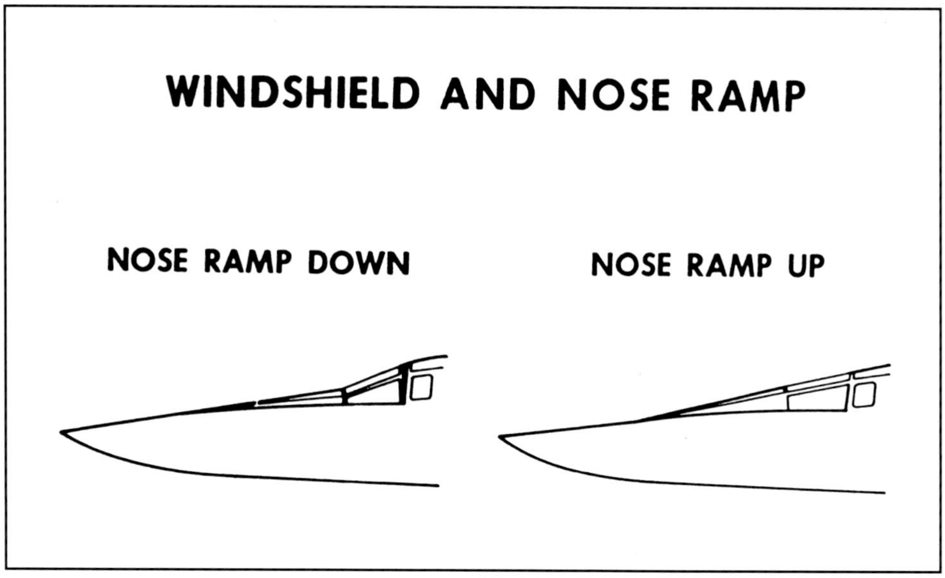

WINDSHIELD AND NOSE RAMP

NOSE RAMP DOWN

NOSE RAMP UP

The operation of the XB-70's nose ramp. At left the nose ramp is lowered to provide greater forward visibility at lower speeds during approach and landing. At right the ramp is raised to improve airflow over the windshield at high speeds. Some forward visibility, although restricted, remains. *AFMC/HO*

Three Valkyries were planned for various research alternatives, #1 being the highest and #7 being the lowest preference. *AFMC/HO*

AIR VEHICLE USAGE ALTERNATIVES
FOLLOW-ON RESEARCH ACTIVITY PREFERENCE

ALTERNATIVE				FOLLOW-ON	
NO.	FLT. HRS	A/V NO.	A/V AVAIL.	PROGRAM CONSIDERATIONS	DESIRABILITY
1	120	1 2 3	X YES YES	NO. 1 AVAIL. FOR STATIC & FATIGUE OR FLT. IF ADDED A/W FLYING DONE	2
2	50	1 2 3	X YES X	A/W OF A/V NOT DEMONSTRATED - ADDED FLYING OF A/V 1 & 3 REQ'D.	4
3	170	1 2 3	YES YES YES	A/V & INSTRUMENTATION SUPPORTS ALL RESEARCH TASKS	1
4	65	1 2 3	X YES YES	SAME AS PROGRAM 2	3
5	75	1 2 3	YES X YES	SIMILAR TO PROGRAM 2 EXCEPT A/V NO.2 NOT AVAILABLE	5
6	180	1 2 3	YES YES X	PREVENTS UTILIZATION OF A/V NO. 3 CAPABILITY	7
7	315	1 2 3	YES YES X	PREVENTS UTILIZAITION OF A/V NO. 3 CAPABILITY	6

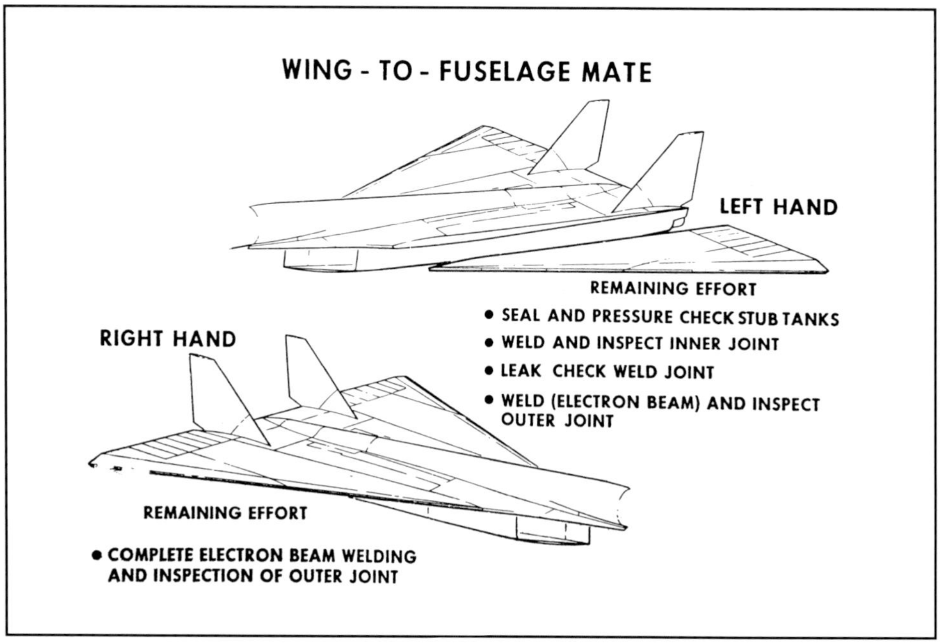

The wing-to-fuselage mating for the XB-70 wing with various steps outlined for inspection. *AFMC/HO*

WING - TO - FUSELAGE MATE

LEFT HAND

REMAINING EFFORT
- SEAL AND PRESSURE CHECK STUB TANKS
- WELD AND INSPECT INNER JOINT
- LEAK CHECK WELD JOINT
- WELD (ELECTRON BEAM) AND INSPECT OUTER JOINT

RIGHT HAND

REMAINING EFFORT
- COMPLETE ELECTRON BEAM WELDING AND INSPECTION OF OUTER JOINT

The B-70's design would use the little-known principle of compression lift to allow the airplane to actually ride on its own sonic shock wave for efficient operation at Mach 3 (2,000 miles per hour). Compression lift was a little-known theory discovered in 1954 during a literature search by A. J. Eggers and C. A. Syverston. The two research scientists worked for NACA (the National Advisory Committee on Aeronautics, now NASA) at Langley Field, Virginia. In 1957, they wrote a technical paper entitled *Aircraft Configurations Developing High Lift/Drag Ratios at High Supersonic Speeds*. It had been stamped Secret and filed away. The paper would provide one of the key answers to the problem of efficiency at Mach speeds. Compression lift was already recognized by some engineers, but what the two NACA engineers suggested was that a high-speed aircraft could actually be designed to take advantage of its own supersonic shock wave by using it to provide lift and use fuel more efficiently. The Lift/Drag ratio could be varied in supersonic flight by relying on the static pressure from the shock wave that formed in front of the splitter and under the wing. North American's new design incorporated the compression lift theory; thus, the XB-70 became one of the most unusual aircraft ever created.

With her unique configuration, size, and power, the XB-70 was a beautiful thing to behold. From her forward canards to her huge vertical twin tails, she looked like a cobra just waiting to strike. Her appearance was kinetic: people who saw her parked on the flight line felt as if she were moving.

The XB-70 is a delta wing aircraft with canards. The canards aided in counteracting the trim changes that were intrinsic to flight at transonic speeds. They increased stability at high angles of attack and allowed for changes to be made without affecting the performance of the delta wing. The canard trailing edges could be lowered up to 25 degrees, which would force the nose up. To compensate, the elevons moved down causing all of the surfaces to lift with nothing being lost from the basic wing lift. This permitted the XB-70 to land at a conventional speed equivalent to commercial jet aircraft. Although canards were a mainstay of the XB-70, in certain configurations they created unstable airflow around the entrances to the engine inlets.

Compression lift was designed into the XB-70 with the wedge-shaped engine box positioned under the wing of the aircraft. This caused positive static pressure behind the main shock wave to react on the large underwing surface. Since there is no effect on the air flowing over the top of the wing to cancel out the resulting lift, at least a 30-percent improvement in lift was available without any increased drag on the aircraft.

The folding wingtips of the XB-70 were another design innovation. They pivoted in flight so they could be folded down for supersonic cruise. This configuration

reduced supersonic directional stability problems, allowed the vertical stabilizers to be smaller than they might otherwise have been, and decreased trim drag at high Mach numbers. There were three positions for the wingtips:

1. Up at subsonic speed.
2. 25 degrees down for low-altitude supersonic flight.
3. 65 degrees down for high-altitude Mach 3 flight.

The XB-70 design had a long, graceful nose that supported a movable nose ramp. Mach 3 flight caused high-drag shock waves at the windshield. North American designed the nose ramp (as part of upper nose surface just ahead of the canopy) to be folded down at low speed, giving pilots a better view for takeoffs and landings. At high-speed cruise, the nose ramp was raised for streamlining, thus reducing drag on the aircraft.

The high temperatures encountered when flying at Mach 2 and Mach 3 made it necessary to build the XB-70 out of something other than standard aircraft aluminum. That "something" was stainless steel honeycomb. The XB-70 was not the first aircraft to be designed with stainless steel honeycomb sandwich panels; the B-58 Hustler had used it in several places earlier on. However, the XB-70's airframe was comprised of at least 69 percent honeycomb material. Powerful as she was, weight was an important constraint. Since the honeycomb material lent itself to light weight, strength, smoothness, fatigue resistance, low heat transfer, and reliability at high temperature, it was considered the prime candidate for the XB-70. North American engineers designed the XB-70's skin so that instead of a single layer, it was a "three-thickness skin," incorporating a 2-inch layer of honeycomb foil between two thin sheets of stainless steel.

The stainless steel honeycomb was expensive to produce in such large quantities as would be required by the XB-70. Special autoclaves had to be built so that the sheets could be heat-treated in larger sizes than had ever been done before. The sheets had to be rolled so thin, down to almost two-thousandths of an inch, to compensate for any additional weight gain. The welding of the sheets together brought with it problems so critical that workers had to wear gloves to prevent oil from their fingertips from interfering with the metals as they were welded together. After cooling, the sheets were inspected by a sonar beam to detect any flaws.

The honeycomb material was used in the wings, engine box, midfuselage, and vertical stabilizers. The stainless steel used was PH15-7 Mo. (molybdenum steel). Titanium was about 8 percent of the total dry weight of 150,000 pounds, used mainly in the forward fuselage. There were actually three types of titanium used. The first was Titanium 6AL-4V, which was heat-treated and used in thicknesses of 0.030 inches to 0.070 inches for the forward fuselage skin and

5387 XB-70A FIRST FLIGHT   21 SEP 64

XB-70 AV-1 looks positively otherworldly in this photo. Note the distance from the ground to the cockpit. *AFMC/HO*

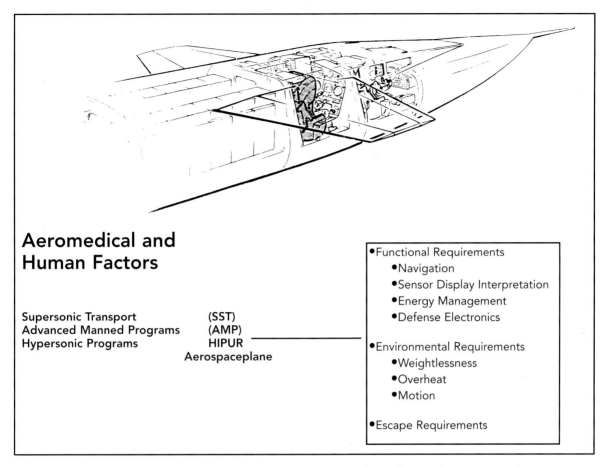

Aeromedical and Human Factors

Supersonic Transport	(SST)
Advanced Manned Programs	(AMP)
Hypersonic Programs	HIPUR
	Aerospaceplane

- Functional Requirements
  - Navigation
  - Sensor Display Interpretation
  - Energy Management
  - Defense Electronics

- Environmental Requirements
  - Weightlessness
  - Overheat
  - Motion

- Escape Requirements

Aeromedical and human factors charts depicting the concerns for cockpit and environmental equipment design. Note the listing for SST, AMP, HIPUR, and Aerospace Plane. *AFMC/HO*

60-foot skin and stringers. The second was 4Al-3Mo-1V, heat-treated to 170,000 pounds/square inch. The third type of titanium, 7A1-4Mo, was used and also heat-treated to 170,000 pounds/square inch. In all, a total of 22,000 titanium parts were used in the XB-70 with 12,000 in the forward fuselage alone. Titanium was also used in the canards main box, the flaps, and vertical stabilizers.

The high temperatures of the engines dictated the use of Rene'41, a high-strength steel with good resistance to fatigue, in the engine compartments. Elsewhere, H-11 tool steel was used for the forward fuselage and fittings. The Valkyrie's nose radome was constructed of a product called Vibran; it was laminated to ensure protection of all the electronics she carried. All of these different metal types, the comprehensive stress analysis, elastic analysis, load factors, and the myriad of other tests that were done during the initial design phase, comprised one of the most ambitious programs in the construction of an airframe. Mach 3 didn't come easy for the Valkyrie, but it would come.

Many of the other systems of the XB-70 were also revolutionary. The "shirt sleeve" environment for pilots was a concept unheard of at the flight speed and altitude that was

marked for the XB-70. The shirt sleeve environment was accomplished mainly by use of a high-pressure bleed air system, supported by Freon refrigeration units. This twofold system maintained the cabin pressure at 8,000 feet. If a rapid decompression occurred due to mechanical or some other failure, the pilots could encapsulate and fly the XB-70 from within clamshell capsules. The refrigeration system relied on two Freon units that helped cool the crew cabin and the equipment bays. These units used high-pressure bleed air to run the Freon compressor turbines. The air entered at 850-degrees Fahrenheit, but by the time the additional bleed air for the fuselage pressurization left the Freon exchangers, the temperature was reduced to 45-degrees Fahrenheit. Any area that was to be cooled actually had tiny holes perforating the walls. Air was then circulated into a glass-lined plenum cell at the end of the porous wall and ducted back to the heat exchangers after passing through a water vaporizer. There was even a provision for a liquid ammonia tank so that the ammonia could be used as a powerful, short-term evaporative coolant as a backup for when the water tank was empty at the end of a long flight. Through all of this, the crew cabin was left at a temperature

35

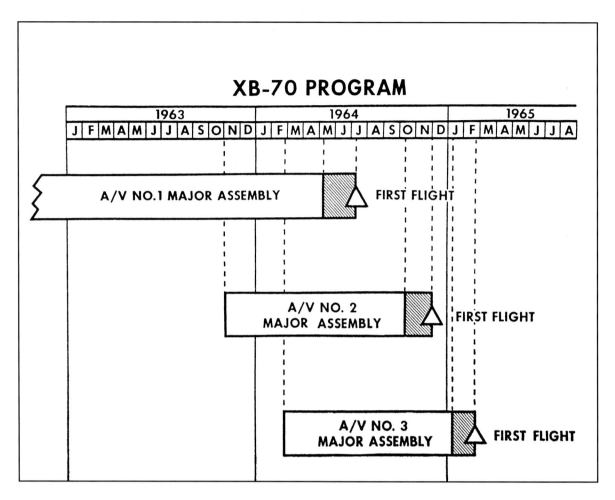

XB-70 PROGRAM

	1963	1964	1965
	J F M A M J J A S O N D	J F M A M J J A S O N D	J F M A M J J A

A/V NO.1 MAJOR ASSEMBLY △ FIRST FLIGHT

A/V NO. 2 MAJOR ASSEMBLY △ FIRST FLIGHT

A/V NO. 3 MAJOR ASSEMBLY △ FIRST FLIGHT

maintained at 70- to 100-degrees Fahrenheit, while the equipment bay was kept at a comfortable 110- to 160-degrees Fahrenheit. There were fuel/water heat exchangers in the number three tank that provided for cooling of landing gear and drag chute compartments by "water walls." It is interesting to note that with all these systems in place, the XB-70 crew flew in regulation pressure suits throughout the program, and only when the remaining Valkyrie was delivered to Wright-Patterson AFB for inclusion in the U.S. Air Force Museum's collection did the pilots fly in regulation flight suits.

The XB-70's fuel system was another unique innovation. The XB-70 had a total of 11 tanks, 3 in each wing and 5 in the fuselage. The third fuselage tank was used to control the flow of the rest of the fuel throughout the aircraft. That tank was installed over the XB-70's center of gravity so that by using the two fuel level valves in that tank, fuel could be transferred to the remaining tanks (via two fuel pumps per tank) to control the trim of the aircraft. Since the fuel system was originally designed as part of the heat sink system, it was protected by 4,000 gallons of water acting as an interim heat sink. This backup allowed water vaporization to extract heat when the fuel could not.

ABOVE: This chart shows the XB-70 development program as planned through the projected first flights of AV-1, AV-2, and AV-3. *AFMC/HO*

RIGHT TOP: A North American Aviation manpower program chart shows the actual and forecast manpower including quality control, tooling, management, and administration. *AFMC/HO*

RIGHT BOTTOM: XB-70 AV-2 major assembly chart showing wing, forward fuselage, forward upper intermediate fuselage, forward lower intermediate fuselage, aft intermediate fuselage, and aft fuselage, with dates and mating schedule. *AFMC/HO*

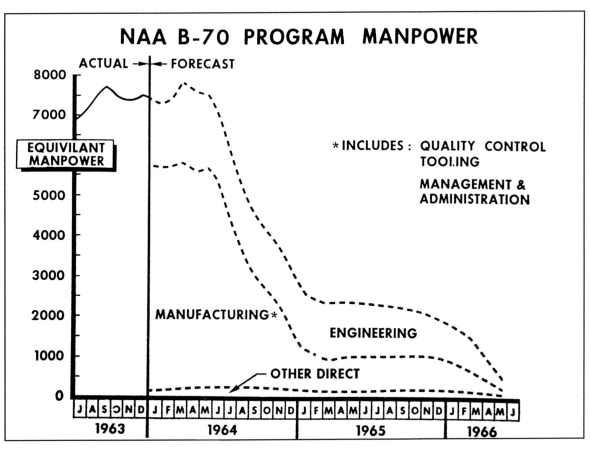

NAA B-70 PROGRAM MANPOWER

ACTUAL → ← FORECAST

EQUIVILANT MANPOWER

*INCLUDES: QUALITY CONTROL
TOOLING

MANAGEMENT &
ADMINISTRATION

MANUFACTURING*

ENGINEERING

OTHER DIRECT

8000
7000
5000
4000
3000
2000
1000
0

J A S O N D | J F M A M J J A S O N D | J F M A M J J A S O N D | J F M A M J
1963 | 1964 | 1965 | 1966

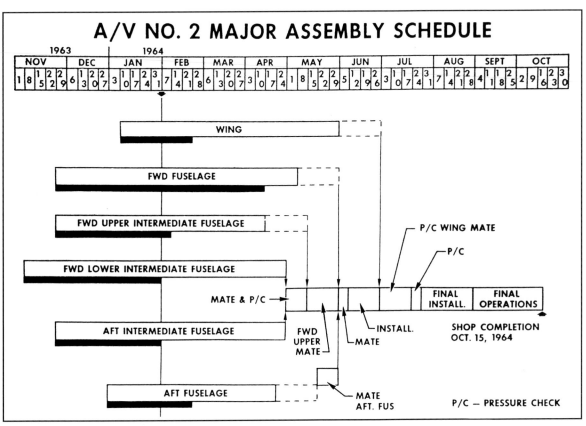

A/V NO. 2 MAJOR ASSEMBLY SCHEDULE

1963			1964							
NOV	DEC	JAN	FEB	MAR	APR	MAY	JUN	JUL	AUG	SEPT	OCT

WING

FWD FUSELAGE

FWD UPPER INTERMEDIATE FUSELAGE

FWD LOWER INTERMEDIATE FUSELAGE

MATE & P/C →

P/C WING MATE

P/C

AFT INTERMEDIATE FUSELAGE

FINAL INSTALL. | FINAL OPERATIONS

FWD UPPER MATE

INSTALL.

MATE

SHOP COMPLETION
OCT. 15, 1964

AFT FUSELAGE

MATE AFT. FUS

P/C — PRESSURE CHECK

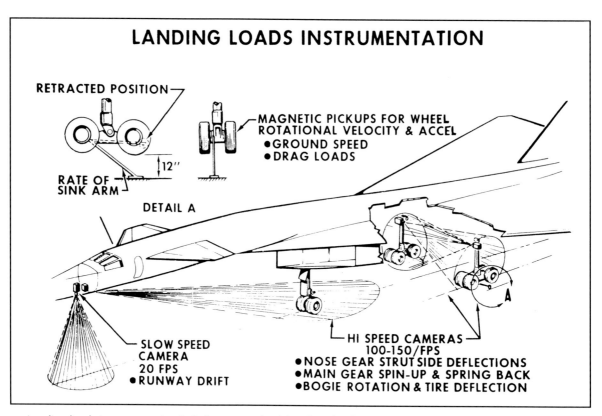

LANDING LOADS INSTRUMENTATION

RETRACTED POSITION

MAGNETIC PICKUPS FOR WHEEL
ROTATIONAL VELOCITY & ACCEL
● GROUND SPEED
● DRAG LOADS

12"

RATE OF
SINK ARM

DETAIL A

SLOW SPEED
CAMERA
20 FPS
● RUNWAY DRIFT

HI SPEED CAMERAS
100-150/FPS
● NOSE GEAR STRUT SIDE DEFLECTIONS
● MAIN GEAR SPIN-UP & SPRING BACK
● BOGIE ROTATION & TIRE DEFLECTION

Landing loads instrumentation includes magnetic pickup for wheel rotational velocity and acceleration; ground speed drag loads; slow-speed camera (20 feet per second); runway drift; high-speed cameras (100-150 feet per second); nose gear strut side deflections, main gear spinup and spring back bogie rotation, and tire deflection. *AFMC/HO*

Close-up of the XB-70's main landing gear bogie and strut. Note the smaller wheel, which is a sensor or wheelspin measuring device for controlling brake actuation, or antiskid functions. *USAF Museum*

North American engineers faced a perplexing problem when tiny pinholes were discovered in the fuel tanks after the first XB-70 (AV-1) was built. Since the JP-6 fuel was pressurized in flight with onboard liquid nitrogen to keep the possibility of explosion to a minimum and to keep tank pressure constant, none of the nitrogen could be allowed to leak. Unfortunately this is exactly what was happening in Valkyrie AV-1. To combat the problem, a DuPont Corporation product called Viton-B was used to seal the pinholes. It was a difficult process at best. The Viton-B had to be applied, then cured for six hours. Hair dryers had to be used to reach the more inaccessible places far back in the tanks. This process was repeated six times, then the tanks were pressurized again for inspection of any more leaks. Tank number five however, being U-shaped and the most difficult to get to inside the aircraft, could never be cured properly, so in Valkyrie AV-1 the tank was shut down and never used. Fueling the XB-70 was a more complex matter than usual. According to the written

The tank section of the XB-70 is lowered into the mating tool to join it with the forward fuselage and aft fuselage. The aft section, built by Avco Corp., was sprayed with a latex-base protective coating. The forward section was mechanically attached and the aft section was welded to the tank sections. *Avco photo via Charles R. Frey*

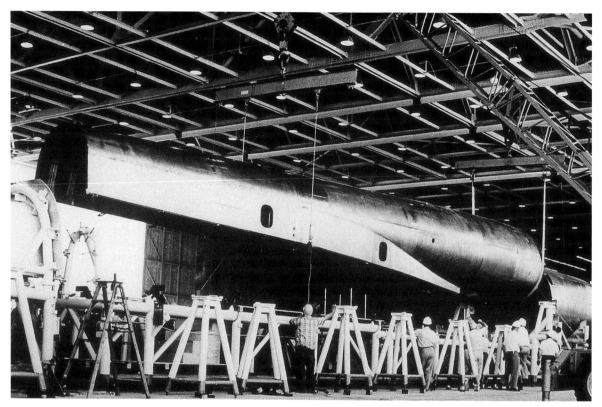

After the fabrication and inspection, the various panels making up the upper forward intermediate fuselage section of the XB-70 are joined by fusion welding in a special weld assembly fixture. Upon completion, the welding areas are closely inspected and X-rayed for any flaws. Rigid quality control requirements are adhered to throughout the entire fabrication of the fuselage structures. *Avco photo, via Charles R. Frey*

procedure, fueling could take one to one-and-one-half hours. The first tanker pumped its load into a second empty tanker; then as the second tanker was being pressurized, dry nitrogen was dribbled in to mix with the JP-6 so that when it finally entered the XB-70 tanks, it was already pressurized with nitrogen and as inert as it could get.

The XB-70 had four major hydraulic systems. These four basic systems led to the subsystems that kept the aircraft going: flight controls, vertical stabilizers, elevons, backup flight controls, wing folds, canard flaps, landing gear, nose wheel steering, wheel brakes, environmental drives, compressors, heat loop pumps, blower fans, flood flow system, emergency generators, drag chute, windshield ramp, engine controls, fuel pumps, and fuel boost. All these systems were controlled by three pumps in a master/slave configuration. The one master pump would control all normal operations, the two slave pumps would remain on for minimum services, such as cooling and lubrication. Should the master pump fail, the two slave pumps would rise to meet the increasing needs. All the primary systems operated as a constant output motor for engine starting. The pump outlets were pressurized through valves for motor operation. During startup, the utility system pumps were depressurized to reduce cranking drag. Engine starting power was supplied by an external ground power unit or, according to early plans, the XB-70 could be made self-sufficient by starting one engine with a cartridge starter, then that engine would provide hydraulic power to the others. The hydraulic starting system saved 380 pounds of weight over that of a system that might normally have been used.

The XB-70 was a large aircraft and needed large landing gear to support her weight. The landing gear weighed more than 12,000 pounds. The main gear had a bogie and a brake stack of 21 stationary discs and 20 revolving discs. The wheels of the XB-70 were made by the B. F. Goodrich company, which also manufactured the brakes. The wheels were connected by bearings directly to the main bogie made of H-11 forged tool steel. An automatic antiskid feature, using a system separate from the main braking system, ensured that there would be no overbraking by the pilot. The XB-70 could

The completed XB-70 master model is used as a mold for casting Avcoramic Unit Tool ceramic platens. After hardening, the ceramic platens are removed from the master model for further finishing before being used for production of honeycomb panels. *Avco photo via Charles R. Frey*

land and take only 45 seconds to stop on a 6,500-foot runway with brakes. The nose wheel configuration was also a new design. Should anything happen while moving down a runway, landing, or taking off, the system would detect the upcoming failure and compensate automatically.

Even something as mundane as hydraulic lines had to be reworked to accommodate the XB-70. If the normal procedure for hydraulic lines had been followed, the XB-70 would have been 10,000 pounds overweight. This led to permanent joints wherever possible, high-strength tubing with temperature tolerance at the high end of the scale, fittings that could be installed without a pinpoint value and anything movable fitted with flexible joints in an all-metal tubing.

Despite all the technological challenges, North American succeeded in most of what it set out to accomplish, leaving some modifications for the second Valkyrie. Much of that had to do with the welding process that had caused so many headaches early in the program. The XB-70 was slowly becoming all she was purported to be: a state-of-the-art, high-speed aircraft.

THE MANNED MISSILE

In 1960, Duell, Sloan, & Pearce published a book entitled *The Manned Missile*. The author was Ed Rees, who had been a military affairs correspondent for *Time* magazine back in the late 1950s. If anyone had a good view of the genre of the times in which the B-70 was born, it was Ed Rees.

In his book, Rees was quick to recognize that there were many critics of the B-70 and that it was easy to understand why. Back then, the concept of the B-70 was alien to conventional post-WW II thinking in the United States. That airplane would climb to an altitude of 15 miles in three minutes, cruise at 2,000 miles per hour (Mach 3), and carry weapons worthy of a ". . . 4,000-mile train load of TNT." According to Rees, the Russians would have to increase their bomber defense spending by six times to counter the B-70 threat. Although the book may seem a bit melodramatic and dated today, it gives one a good feeling for the times, an idea of how little the bomber gap was really understood, and the flavor of the era during which all this took place.

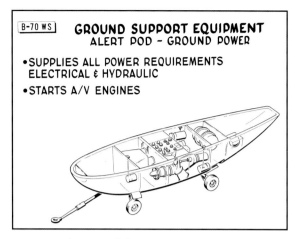

GROUND SUPPORT EQUIPMENT
ALERT POD - GROUND POWER

• SUPPLIES ALL POWER REQUIREMENTS ELECTRICAL & HYDRAULIC

• STARTS A/V ENGINES

A rare drawing of the proposed ground support alert pod that would have enabled the XB-70 to be scrambled from alert in three minutes. Note that it was designed to supply all power requirements electric and hydraulic and to start the engines. *Courtesy AFMC/HO*

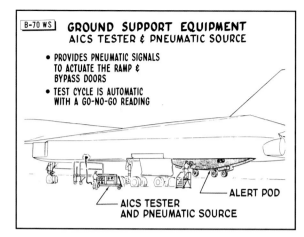

GROUND SUPPORT EQUIPMENT
AICS TESTER & PNEUMATIC SOURCE

• PROVIDES PNEUMATIC SIGNALS TO ACTUATE THE RAMP & BYPASS DOORS

• TEST CYCLE IS AUTOMATIC WITH A GO-NO-GO READING

AICS TESTER AND PNEUMATIC SOURCE — ALERT POD

The projected uses for other ground support equipment like the AICS tester and a good view of the position for the alert pod to be attached under the engine bay. *AFMC/HO*

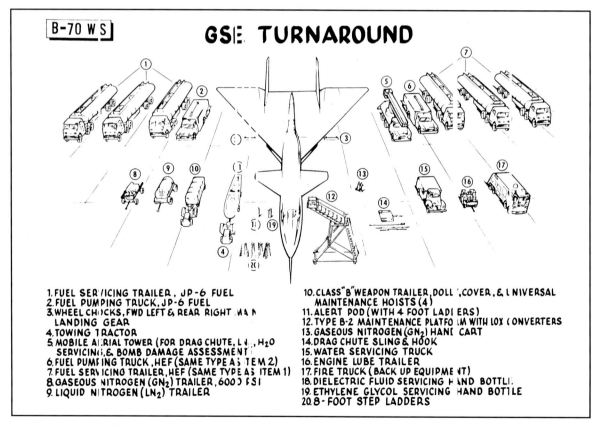

B-70 WS

GSE TURNAROUND

1. FUEL SERVICING TRAILER, JP-6 FUEL
2. FUEL PUMPING TRUCK, JP-6 FUEL
3. WHEEL CHOCKS, FWD LEFT & REAR RIGHT MAIN LANDING GEAR
4. TOWING TRACTOR
5. MOBILE AERIAL TOWER (FOR DRAG CHUTE, LN₂, H₂O SERVICING, & BOMB DAMAGE ASSESSMENT)
6. FUEL PUMPING TRUCK, HEF (SAME TYPE AS ITEM 2)
7. FUEL SERVICING TRAILER, HEF (SAME TYPE AS ITEM 1)
8. GASEOUS NITROGEN (GN₂) TRAILER, 6000 PSI
9. LIQUID NITROGEN (LN₂) TRAILER
10. CLASS "B" WEAPON TRAILER, DOLLY, COVER, & UNIVERSAL MAINTENANCE HOISTS (4)
11. ALERT POD (WITH 4 FOOT LADDERS)
12. TYPE B-2 MAINTENANCE PLATFORM WITH LOX CONVERTERS
13. GASEOUS NITROGEN (GN₂) HAND CART
14. DRAG CHUTE SLING & HOOK
15. WATER SERVICING TRUCK
16. ENGINE LUBE TRAILER
17. FIRE TRUCK (BACK UP EQUIPMENT)
18. DIELECTRIC FLUID SERVICING HAND BOTTLE
19. ETHYLENE GLYCOL SERVICING HAND BOTTLE
20. 8-FOOT STEP LADDERS

A very rare line drawing showing the projected service accoutrements for the B-70 had she been fielded. *AFMC/HO*

 **EMPLOYEE REPORT**

SEPTEMBER, 1964

NORTH AMERICAN AVIATION, INC.

SPACE-AGE MILESTONES: XB-70 IN MAKING

POISED — North American's XB-70A, manufactured by the Los Angeles Division, is poised proudly on the flight line during final preparations for first flight at Palmdale plant. At right is view of aft engine section of triple-sonic craft. Shot was taken during late night tests at Palmdale facility.

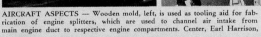

AIRCRAFT ASPECTS — Wooden mold, left, is used as tooling aid for fabrication of engine splitters, which are used to channel air intake from main engine duct to respective engine compartments. Center, Earl Harrison, LA B-70 Enginering, reviews main landing gear shock struts. At right is phase of ground vibration test, which was conducted to determine structural stiffness of air vehicle No. 1 and to determine in-flight flutter boundaries.

WING WORK — Fabricated aft intermediate test specimen, shown with workmen, was used to test wing bending, simulated loads in duct region, and for fuel tank verification. Here men prepare to move completed section into Structures Lab. Right picture demonstrates unusual configuration of XB-70A wing as men on top perform series of actuator tests. When craft reaches higher Mach numbers, wing tips fold down to achieve flight stability.

43

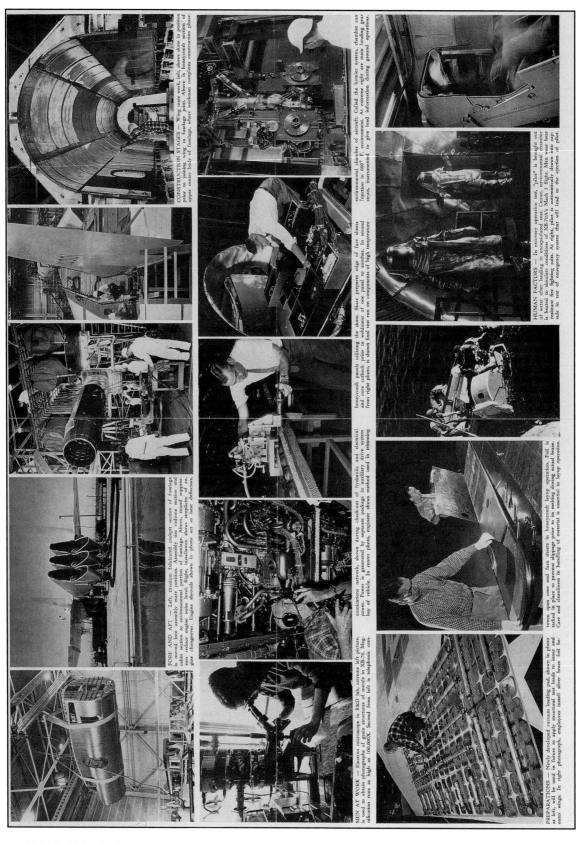

ABOVE, PREVIOUS PAGE AND OPPOSITE: This newsletter was put out by North American Aviation heralding the XB-70 and her development at Plant 42. *Boeing Corp/ North American Aviation*

FOCAL POINT — XB-70A dominates Palmdale facility. At left is bow-on view. At right, pre-flight crews work on aircraft in early morning hours.

TOUCHING UP — Viton high temperature sealant is brushed over weldment and brazed joints to seal fuel tanks. Center, electrical discharge cutting, trimming, and grinding tool was used extensively in XB-70 construction. Photo demonstrates the cutting of hole through honeycomb panel. At right, heat tests are conducted on simulated section of crew compartment in Environmental Simulator of R&D Aerospace Labs in temperatures reaching 500° F.

CLOSEUPS — Portable X-ray equipment, like that in left photo, enabled Quality Control personnel to move from site to site and X-ray all welded joints. In center picture, Gary Stroh, vice-president and general manager of B-70 division, examines the largest honeycomb panel fabricated for program. At right, landing gear operation is demonstrated. Folding operation comes prior to retraction of landing gear into the wheel well area above.

"HOME" OF XB-70A — Photograph shows full length of Los Angeles Division's XB-70A as it waits for first flight in hangar where it was built at Palmdale.

CHAPTER 4

Night photo of the XB-70 being prepared for an engine test. Note the large funnels connected to the engine ducts for sound suppression. *GE Aircraft Engines*

Engine Design

The seed that was planted back in 1955, and eventually became the engine to power the XB-70, was originally conceived of by General Electric and North American Aviation and was known as the J-79-X275. This designation meant that the engine could reach Mach 2.75. The J-79-X275 was to be created for interceptor "study," and even back then it was casually implied that the engine could possibly make it to Mach 3.

At the time, the U.S. Air Force was already funding two study projects with Pratt & Whitney and Allison engines (the J-91 and the J-89 respectively). The contract had been presumed won by Allison engines, but because the specifications for the new bomber had been changed, General Electric, with the help of some unique design changes, landed the contract in May 1957. Contract in hand, their J-79-X275 became the YJ-93.

Their engine was to be the powerplant for the XB-70 as well as the F-108 interceptor, and it was also to be the world's first supersonic engine to work continuously at Mach 3.

There were other plans for the YJ-93 engine. Some of the concepts suggested included use in fighters and attack aircraft because the engine could provide small frontal area, high takeoff thrust, low weight, and high-speed performance. The engine was also considered for use in the Vertical Takeoff and Landing (VTOL) program because of its low weight, control flexibility, and high-temperature cycle capability. The YJ-93 might also have been suitable for powering air-breathing boosters because of its acceleration and thrust in the transonic speed range, high Mach capability, and high-altitude capability—qualities that would be useful for recoverable missile launchers. In addition, the YJ-93 would likely be an excellent candidate for a planned SST because of its high supersonic capability and a purported low takeoff noise. Although it was later learned that the YJ-93 was as noisy as any other engine in its class, no real mention of noise level was ever discussed during the program because the engine was classified, and thrust could be determined by noise level in decibels.

When the first engine went into test in September of 1958, it took with it some original design changes. Once again, the XB-70 was going to bring to the world a new way of designing turbine blades. General Electric came up with the theory and the proficiency of electrolytically drilling air cooling holes longitudinally in the large turbine blades. This was known as "STEM" drilling and General Electric went on to use it in many of its engines. The YJ-93 also had variable compressor stators, a three-main-bearing design, and a new overall lightweight design that contributed to the decision to use it in the B-70 program.

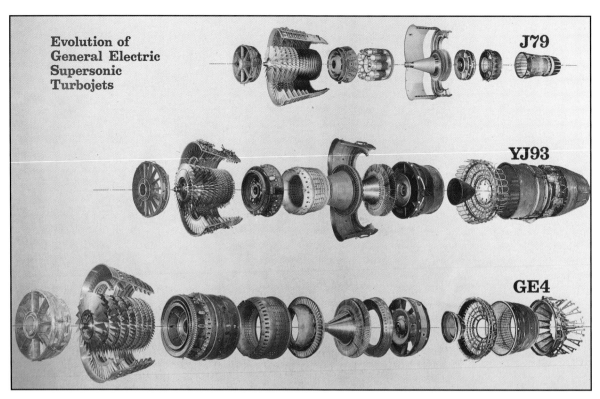

These exploded views depict the evolution of the J-79 engine to the YJ-93, then to the GE4. *GE Aircraft Engines*

The YJ-93-3 "six-pack" design was conceptual. It was the first time that engines were placed together in a box design. These engines were fed by two inlet ducts, three engines for each duct, under the XB-70 fuselage. While simple in form, many things had to be overcome in the domain of triplesonic flight. It was obvious from the beginning that fuel and heat were going to be a big concern. Mach 3 flight produced a lot of heat, so the time had come to think about the fuel as a heat sink. The current fuel being used was JP-4, a standard fuel that produced high vapor pressure. It would not be suitable for the XB-70, so JP-6 was developed with lower vapor pressure and better thermal stability (and therefore its resistance to autogenous ignition), tolerance of high temperatures, and good heat sink capabilities.

Autogenous ignition is defined as automatic ignition or explosion of a fuel that is subjected to aerodynamic heating of the fuel tanks. The ability of the heat sink to function relied on temperature differential between the fuel and the inlet fuel-temperature limit. The temperature limit of 750-degrees Fahrenheit at the engine inlet was established early in the B-70 development stage and was based on fuel thermal stability. Air temperatures at Mach 3 would definitely prevent a standard fuel from being used as a cooling mechanism. Tests were done to make sure that JP-6 would be reliable at high temperatures. It was found that the fuel was not quite stable enough at these high temperatures, so inclusion of a fuel cooling water (flash tanks) boiler system provided extra heat sink capability.

When the XB-70 came into being, it allowed engine and airframe design to be integrated for the first time. The engine designers did not have to worry about the other aircraft that could have been designated to fly with the YJ-93, hence it provided more freedom for innovation. Although considered for other uses, the YJ-93 was developed solely for the XB-70 and the F-108. The prototype XJ-93-1 slated for the F-108 could produce 27,200 pounds of thrust, while the YJ-93-3 produced 28,000 pounds of thrust for the XB-70.

The engine box design helped simplify installation. Any of the six engines could be interchanged at any time. One of the B-70's selling points was the fact that an engine could be changed on the flight line in 25 minutes. When General Electric designed the YJ-93 for the "six-pack" design of engine box, it led to a radical change in engine installation. The design utilized six ball-ended links that supported the transmittal of loads from the engine to the airframe without introducing negative effects on either.

A further breakthrough was an innovative engine-mounted shroud that was developed to protect the aircraft from the heat of the aft combustors. The shroud was installed around the afterburner and had its inner surface coated with .008 inches of gold plating to reflect afterburner heat back to the engine, thus protecting the engine

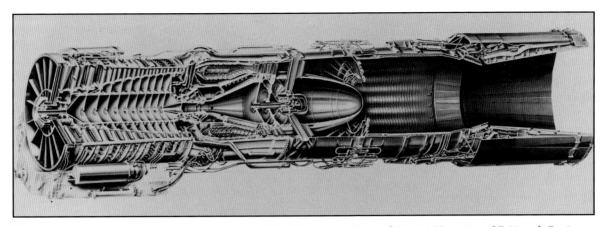

This color cutaway illustration shows in some detail the internal workings of the YJ-93 engine. *GE Aircraft Engines*

The preflight for the XB-70 began late at night and ran well into the morning hours as illustrated in this night shot. *GE Aircraft Engines*

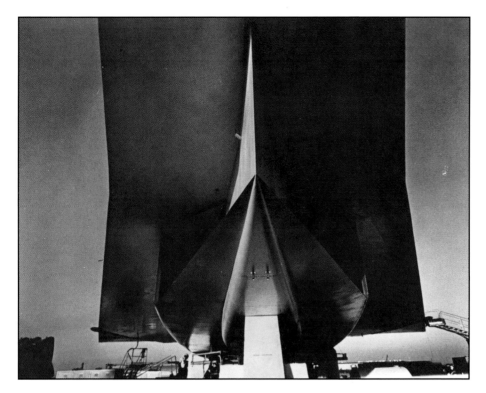

This close-up view shows the unique splitter that controlled the air flowing through the XB-70's engine inlets. Each inlet delivered air to three of the XB-70's six YJ-93 engines. The inlets were critical to the efficient functioning of the engines. *GE Aircraft Engines*

bay from damage. By utilizing the shroud and holding the aircraft structure outside it to an 800-degree temperature limit, there was a great weight savings in comparison to an unshrouded setup.

INLET SYSTEM

One of the more revolutionary pieces of technology used in the XB-70 was the engine inlet system. When designing inlet ducts to support supersonic compression, one must consider many aerodynamic theories. For the XB-70 designers, it was virgin territory, and they didn't have super fast computers and design programs to help them with the wind tunnel tests that designers have today.

The inlets were large and featured variable geometry control, known as the air induction control system (AICS). The XB-70 had two ducts that fed three engines each. In each duct, nearly 90 percent of the compressed air was fed through what was essentially a 6-foot high, 80-foot long tunnel that tapered down to the same height as the engine inlets, while the remaining air circumvented the compressor via bypass doors and was dumped back into the exhaust stream. At Mach 3 at 65,000 feet (the design point condition), air compressed as it traveled down the duct until the engine inlet pressure came to about 30 psi. This method of controlling the inlet air is unlike the method used on the SR-71, which employs a conical spike that regulates the

throat pressures fore and aft and helps to position the shock for changes in Mach speed. On the SR-71, compression takes place both inside and outside the inlet. The spike controls the ratio of inlet capture area to the throat area. The forward bypass controls the location of the terminal (normal) shock. The difference between both the XB-70 and the SR-71 was that the XB-70 had two-dimensional inlets with variable geometry walls and the SR-71 used axisymmetric inlets with movable spikes.

When the SR-71 takes off or lands, or is otherwise flying at low speed, the spike is forward to regulate subsonic air flow to the engine. The spike is retracted when at cruise speed to position the supersonic shock wave just ahead of the engine. In the XB-70, the inlet was made to reduce the air velocity so that the main positive shock wave was made by the wedge-shaped splitter just forward of the inlets and continued aft to the throat area near the engine faces. If the inlet pressure became too great, the shock waves were expulsed from the inlet and produced a condition known as an "unstart." Unstarts would not shut down the engine, but they would dramatically increase drag, so much so that it would buffet the entire aircraft.

Unstarts could also result in what was known as "duct buzz." Duct buzz occurred when a shock wave bounced in and out of the duct in rapid oscillation. It resulted in pressure changes inside the inlets that could be detrimental to the structure and reduce high-speed flight due to the oscillating, unbalanced side forces in the duct and loss of engine thrust.

Thus, the inlets were designed to control the shock waves encountered in supersonic flight so that they would

LEFT: The large YJ-93 engine is shown here being worked on at the General Electric plant at Evendale, Ohio. *GE Aircraft Engines*

A YJ-93 engine being inspected at the General Electric's Evendale plant. *GE Aircraft Engines*

not be "swallowed" by the YJ-93 engines. If the shock waves were to reach the engines, the engines would become useless. They would be unable to produce thrust because of disturbances produced by the resultant high-speed, low-pressure air. The shock waves were manipulated by mechanically changing the shape of the inlet ducts in flight. By moving the inlet ramps in a certain way, depending upon speed and altitude, the shock waves could be held stationary in the ducts at some point before reaching the engine faces. Between the shock wave and the engines, the air would slow to subsonic speeds but increase in pressure to as much as 30 times that of the air ahead of the shock waves.

The YJ-93s could handle the high-pressure, low-speed air quite well because jet engines are designed to compress incoming air before feeding it to the area where combustion takes place and thrust is produced. All air fed into the engine passed through the engine. So, part of the inlet system, in addition to being able to

change its shape, had a series of bypass doors that could be used to direct excess air around the engine in an efficient fashion. This allowed air flow through the engine with less compression, thus creating a lower compression ratio, which ultimately reduced the work load of the YJ-93, yet permitted full airflow to the afterburner. This was actually a "pseudo-ramjet."

The operation of the mechanism controlling the inlet system and the bypass doors was critical. Positions of the various components had to be changed to match the airplane's speed, the engine settings, altitude, and air temperature. With so many variables, the shape of the inlet system and the position of the bypass doors were almost constantly changing. In modern operational aircraft, the inlet system and its associated systems are manipulated automatically. That was not so in the first XB-70. In that aircraft, the copilot made all the changes manually, through the inlet controls available to him in the cockpit, relying on his instruments and the flight plan to tell him how to manipulate

YJ-93 engine being readied for testing. *GE Aircraft Engines*

the system. At high Mach speeds, the copilot of XB-70 AV-1 was a busy crew member indeed. In XB-70 AV-2, the inlet duct system was automatically controlled.

FUEL MANAGEMENT

Fuel management relates to the way the crew of an aircraft "manages" or uses the fuel carried aloft with the airplane. For the simplest aircraft, fuel management means making sure the engine has enough fuel to keep it operating long enough for the airplane to take off, fly for the requisite length of time, and then land safely. The general rule in such cases is: "Don't run out of gas while still in the air."

Most aircraft carry fuel in more than one tank. The purpose of this is to distribute the weight of the fuel conveniently—and more or less evenly—while carrying enough to give the aircraft a satisfactory range. In many of the smaller airplanes, it is normal for fuel to be carried in tanks within the wings, or in older aircraft one may find a fuel tank in the fuselage.

Wherever the fuel tanks are placed in the aircraft, the flight characteristics are affected to some degree as the fuel is consumed. With tanks in the fuselage, consumption will change the pitch trim of the aircraft. With a tank in each wing, it may be possible to draw fuel from both tanks at the same time, or it may be necessary to alternate the tanks from which fuel is drawn during flight in order to maintain a comfortable roll stability. Otherwise, the airplane may tend to turn in the direction of the heavier wing, requiring corrective trim.

If there are two or more tanks in each wing, for example, it is generally recommended to draw fuel from the outer tanks first because the weight in them is farther from the center of gravity. However, in some circumstances, this may not be true since outboard fuel does provide wing bending relief, as in the case of the U-2 where outboard fuel is used last. If the system is designed to draw fuel automatically from both wings at the same time, usually the outer tanks will feed the inner tanks, thus maintaining balance. In some aircraft,

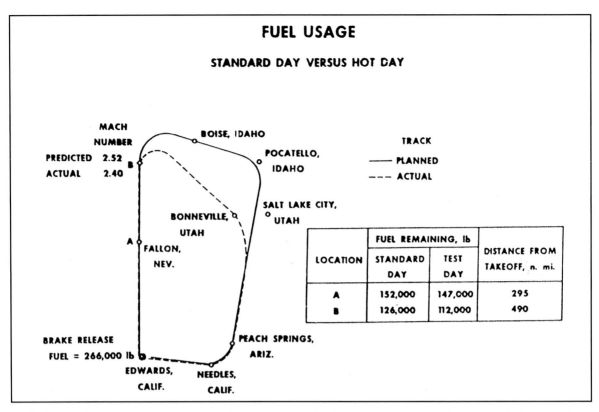

FUEL USAGE

STANDARD DAY VERSUS HOT DAY

	MACH NUMBER			
PREDICTED	2.52			
ACTUAL	2.40			

TRACK
— PLANNED
--- ACTUAL

BOISE, IDAHO
POCATELLO, IDAHO
SALT LAKE CITY, UTAH
BONNEVILLE, UTAH
FALLON, NEV.
A
B

LOCATION	FUEL REMAINING, lb		DISTANCE FROM TAKEOFF, n. mi.
	STANDARD DAY	TEST DAY	
A	152,000	147,000	295
B	126,000	112,000	490

BRAKE RELEASE
FUEL = 266,000 lb

PEACH SPRINGS, ARIZ.
EDWARDS, CALIF.
NEEDLES, CALIF.

Fuel usage for the XB-70 on a standard day versus a hot day. Note the 26,000-pound difference between estimated and actual consumption. *AFMC/HO*

however, the pilot must manage the fuel distribution by periodically using valves to switch tanks to maintain trim.

As with many sophisticated aircraft, the XB-70 relied upon the shifting of fuel throughout its system of tanks to maintain the correct balance of the airframe as it flew. Placement of the center of gravity depended upon the speed and altitude at which the aircraft was flown at any given time. Any change in the flight regime was likely to require a corresponding change in the placement of the fuel's weight within the aircraft. Thus, movement of part of the bulk of fuel, fore, aft, starboard, and port was done with pumps and was crucial to keeping the airplane stable.

In the XB-70 AV-1, the fuel management was done by the copilot who controlled the pumps and valves manually through a series of cockpit controls. Had later production versions of the aircraft been flown, most of the fuel transfer activity would have been relegated to an automatic fuel management system. In this case, the pilot in charge of managing the fuel system would simply monitor the automatic system, and only intervene under special conditions if the need arose.

DEVELOPMENT OF JP-6 AND ZIP FUEL

It should be mentioned here just how much time was spent on developing what was known as HEF, that is High Energy Fuel, better known as ZIP fuel. Any range extension on the XB-70 would have been a blessing and it was

sought after in many ways. Range extension superseded even Mach speed when it came to the development of an intercontinental bomber. The advantages of HEF were deemed critical because of the limited operational status of the air-to-air refueling tanker system the Air Force was using. HEF could increase target coverage for a B-70 bomber and reduce the reliance of tanker support. Some of the fuel formulations that were being looked at were metal slurries (especially magnesium), liquid hydrogen, and three types of boron-based fuels.

Researchers found that when boron was used in the afterburner, it increased range by 16 percent. If it was used in the primary combustor and the afterburner, it could increase range by at least 30 percent. Another boron-based fuel, alkylborane also had promise, although it involved a new field of chemistry that was yet unknown and untried. It weighed about the same as JP fuel and took up the same amount of volume, but produced at least 40 percent more energy. Finally, boron oxide, a viscous liquid fuel that would melt at about 900-degrees Fahrenheit and stayed fluid to temperatures over 3,000-degrees Fahrenheit, held some useful properties as well.

General Electric and the Navy had begun studying boron-based fuels way back in the mid-1940s. The Navy's active boron fuel program, known as "Project ZIP," was developed by Callery Chemical and Olin Mathieson

This rendered drawing shows the XB-70 taking off from Edwards AFB, CA. Note the black exhaust plume trailing in the distance. *AFMC/HO*

Chemical. Callery was the first to produce alkylated borane and ethyl decaborane in November of 1953, while General Electric conducted its tests as a subcontractor to Olin Matheison. The Air Force took over the small General Electric concern for $178,000, and created a small-scale fuel evaluation project known as " DASH," which led to the first effort to extrapolate small-scale lab studies of the development concept in a dual-fuel J-79-type afterburner, which General Electric described as "PROJECT ZOOM."

PROJECT ZOOM had many technical problems to solve, including developing high-temperature bearings and coatings, figuring out how to store the fuel, minimizing the fuel's spontaneous ignition hazard, and creating a dual-fuel system for the engine. The new silicon bearings and silicate coating had to be developed for use in the engine to withstand temperatures over 2,300-degrees Fahrenheit. Fuel storage was a challenging issue, because the fuel was 10 times as toxic as cyanide and would solidify after a time at high temperature, with any sort of moisture and oxygen

tossed in to hasten the process. Having the fuel solidify wasn't a problem with full fuel tanks, but anything less than that could harden up in no time at all. More of a problem was the fuel's susceptibility to spontaneous ignition. It would ignite with little provocation, especially excessive exposure to air, contaminants, and static electricity. Since the entire system was to be a dual-fuel system, it required that JP-6 and the ZIP fuel be compatible. The dual-fuel system would also add 300 pounds of weight to each of the engines and 220 pounds to each afterburner, for a total of 3,120 pounds to the aircraft.

Even though the concept of ZIP fuels was making progress, it was still in its infancy and the problems of trying to produce a sufficient quantity of the material, high production costs, and difficulty of handling the fuel made it appear to be hopeless. Ultimately, the ZIP fuel project didn't produce the results needed to field it, so it was ultimately shut down, causing a six-month delay in the J93-GE-5 engine program. The J93-GE-5 was canceled on July 16, 1959, ending the program of ZIP fuels for the B-70.

CHAPTER 5

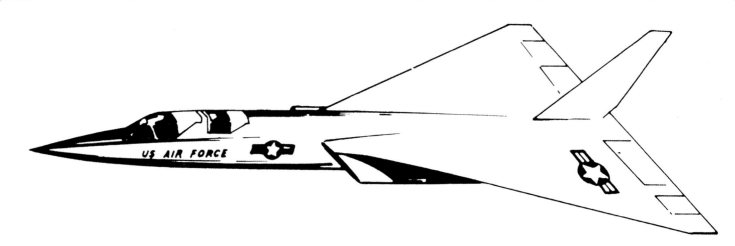

F-108:J93

This is a rare concept drawing by GE aircraft engines depicting the F-108 Rapier. *GE Aircraft Engines*

Defensive Systems

B-70 DEFENSIVE SYSTEMS

Although speed was the Valkyrie's main defense against enemy missiles and interceptors, the bombers included what was called an "active defense system," which was comprised of decoys to lead hostile aircraft and missiles astray along with radar-seeking missiles to destroy whatever got past the decoys.

In August 1958 North American's B-70 project office at Wright-Patterson AFB submitted a proposal for the B-70 weapons system program plan that suggested that the bomber carry such an active defense subsystem. The company's intent was to find out if the so-called active defense concept was really feasible. An evaluation would have to be done to establish whether such a subsystem could be efficiently installed in the aircraft, and how it would affect the bomber's performance and the probability of mission success. North American embarked upon a special "Active Defense Feasibility Study" as part of the development program. The study was completed in March 1959.

With the defense missile now considered an important factor in the bomber's development, North American looked at three basic types of missiles for use in the B-70: a "lenticular" missile, a "cylindrical" missile, and a modified GAR-9. The lenticular missile was a very unorthodox lens-shaped device resembling "nothing so much as a flying saucer" that was being developed at the Wright Air Development Center (WADC) as an element of the Defensive Antimissile System (DAMS). The cylindrical missile had a canard configuration and was designed to follow a preprogrammed launch course and employ a midcourse and terminal infrared homing guidance system. The GAR-9, later to be used in the YF-12, was a highly advanced conventional missile with a delta planform and radar homing guidance.

Of the three, the cylindrical missile appeared to be the most lucrative for the B-70's defense. It weighed less than the others, had more range, and used superior guidance techniques. It did not depart radically from existing programs, and its development was thought to present few risks.

North American had been working on the assumption that, due to the B-70's speed, any real threat to the aircraft would come from its forward hemisphere; that is, from in front of the bomber. In that case, the cylindrical missile would be suitable for defense against enemy attacks. However, should the enemy develop an interceptor with a Mach 3 capability, the bomber would have to defend itself against threats from all directions, which would require spherical coverage. In that case, the lenticular missile presented "an appealing growth potential."

The Air Force published Standard Aircraft Characteristics charts on the North American F-108 while it was in the conceptual stage. These charts were commonly compiled from Air Force and contractor data. *USAF Museum*

Standard Aircraft Characteristics

AUTHORITY OF
E SECRETARY
THE AIR FORCE

F-108A
RAPIER
North American

TWO J93-GE-3 AF

GENERAL ELECTRI

The question of what kind of defense coverage a bomber ought to have is really a very old one. It goes back to the 1930s, when the concept of a truly long-range strategic bombing platform was being brought to reality. World War I bombers had carried defensive armament, but there was no experience to show how to apply World War I ideas to the vastly improved bombers on the drawing boards a decade and a half later. A good example was the Boeing 299, first tested in 1935. It was very fast for its day. In fact, it was widely believed to be faster than any operational fighter in existence at the time; therefore, attack from the rear was thought to be impossible. Accordingly, the early model B-17s could fire forward, to each side, up, and down, but not directly to the rear. Of course, new fighters were being designed at the same time and, not surprisingly, one of their most important features was greater speed. It wasn't until the B-17E—first flown in September 1941—was introduced that tail guns became part of the defensive armament package of the "Flying Fortress." Somewhere along the line, Army Air Corps officials realized that the 1935 design was no longer the fastest thing in the sky, and defense from the rear was needed. Thus, the B-17 finally acquired what came to be known as "spherical defense."

The enemy threats against which the B-70 would need spherical defense were thought to be, (a) a Mach 3 interceptor fighter armed with an advanced missile similar to the USAF's GAR-9; (b) an advanced, high-speed, area defense surface-to-air missile (SAM); or (c), a combination thereof. North American believed that to protect the bomber adequately, five to eight defensive missiles would be sufficient to give a "sizable improvement" in survivability over no defense at all—provided a system could be installed with little or no range penalty. However, estimates predicted that either a GAR-9 or a cylindrical missile would cause a range reduction of 675 nautical miles. With the lenticular defense missile the range might be reduced as much as 780 nautical miles. If the range reduction could be tolerated, the bomber's ability to penetrate enemy defenses successfully might be increased by up to 10 percent.

SR-197 STUDY

Back in January 1959, the Air Research and Development Command (ARDC) advised that additional defensive antimissile research would not be tied to the B-70 program unless the B-70 Project Office requested it. A study requirement had been issued to discover what type of new penetration aids bombers would need in the future. The prime contractor apparently felt that the B-70 could survive and operate effectively while relying upon all the currently programmed defensive subsystems then available. Other contractors argued for suitable additions to the basic defense systems then contemplated.

An evaluation of the SR-197 study reached four conclusions:

a. SR-197 was a study to determine the need for penetration aids for the B-70 and the study of decoys and antiradar missiles for possible use with other B-70 defensive subsystems.

b. The only contractor who really evaluated active defensive missiles had rated them as decoys.

c. An active defense missile system is the only practicable and effective penetration aid presently known to defeat a nuclear warhead without detonation.

d. The effects of detonated nuclear warheads on the B-70 aircraft formation had not been adequately demonstrated. The results of the study could indicate that the Bomber Defense Missile approach may have a very significant advantage over other means of defense.

The Project Office clearly wanted both types of defensive systems for the B-70—both ECM and defensive missiles. Thus, in its evaluation of the SR-197 study, the Project Office advocated the two options and came down solidly on both sides of the question! As they saw it, the proper defensive array for the B-70 would consist of interceptor missiles, chaff-dispensing vehicles, track-breaking missiles to counter infrared and radar-homing enemy missiles, and ECM systems. In other words, everything possible to cover all options. All of these systems would have to be carried on the bomber at the expense of its ability to deliver its offensive weapons load: nuclear bombs.

The creation of the defensive systems never got beyond the study stage. On December 1, 1959, the Air Force directed that the B-70 program be limited to the "development of one air vehicle" to be an experimental aircraft with no military capability. The contractors for subsystems were so notified, the contracts were terminated, and many of the studies were abandoned or put on the back burner. The Air Force left the door open for later resumption by stating, "Should the program resume its status as the source of a successor vehicle to contemporary strategic bombers, the matter would again become current."

The matter of developing defensive systems seems to be a perennial stumbling block for those working on the design of a new bomber. After the B-52 and the B-58, both of which had tailgun installations as well as Electronic Counter Measure (ECM) defenses, no further consideration seems to have been given to any type of active defensive armament, likely for good reasons. Modern supersonic and/or stealthy bombers could not make use of gun turrets and remain stealthy. Defensive interceptor missiles might be possible, but combining them with strategic or tactical ordnance requires a tremendous increase in complexity that is not compatible with the bomber's mission. Thus, in the modern world, bomber defense has been relegated either to passive or active electronic defensive measures exclusively.

The B-1 relies upon stealthy design and ECM for defense and the same holds true even more so for the B-2. Speed and stealthiness provide a large degree of protection while electronics provides the rest, in varying degrees. Yet, both the B-1 and the B-2 apparently had problems with ECM effectiveness. Their problems were somewhat the same as had been experienced in the B-70 program. Air Force planners are known for the tendency to load capabilities on a new design without much regard for practicality—and then expect all the new goodies they have asked for to work perfectly. The people who design and build airplanes and their subsystems know that it doesn't work that way. Every new capability requires a compromise, and compromise means that nothing is ever 100 percent effective. On top of that, the customer—in this case the Air Force—wants to make sure it's getting its money's worth as well as meeting schedules.

THE F-108 RAPIER

The B-70 and the F-108 were supposed to share the same technology. In actuality, the F-108 was really a downsized version of the B-70. The idea of developing the F-108 as an off-shoot of the B-70 was a cost-saving measure. Money would have been saved if both aircraft used the same basic engine, the same stainless steel honeycomb airframe materials, the same hydrogen-purged fuel system, and the same clamshell crew escape capsules.

The main mission of the F-108 was to deter armed attack against the United States and North America by providing the maximum defense potential against all airborne threats in the post-1962 world. The Rapier would have been built as a long-range polar interceptor capable of intercepting Soviet flights over the North Pole and protecting U.S. air space. This defense function was to employ the F-108's potential to search out, evaluate, and destroy these hostile penetrators at ranges beyond the capabilities of other defense systems. The F-108 was designed to operate not only in conjunction with other weapons systems, but also to operate well beyond the bounds of ground environment surveillance. It was designed to operate autonomously, and to rely upon its self-contained high-performance search, navigation, and communications equipment.

In times of war, F-108 operations would have included directed intercepts and organized search missions that would have resulted in repeated attacks with up to three kills per interceptor. Operating beyond SAGE (Semi-Automatic Ground Environment), the F-108 was to have made positive identification of DEW (Distant Early Warning) line violations, attack and trail hostile raiders through remote zones, and report directly via long-range radio. Operating within the ZI (Zone of the Interior), the F-108A's performance features of all-weather capability, long range at Mach 3, and 15-minute turnarounds, permitted flexible commitment of forces to achieve the precise concentration of power required at any battle area with maximum retention of reserves.

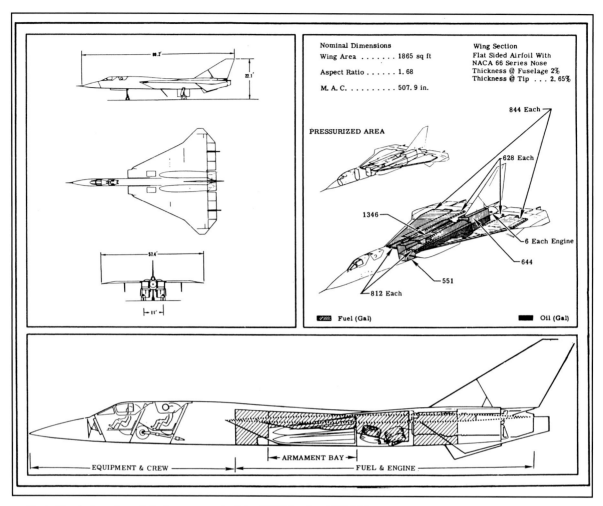

Early North American Aviation proposal of the F108 Rapier. *USAF Museum*

The F-108A was to have carried two crewmen and internally stowed missile armament. As originally conceived, this high-performance air vehicle was to have cruised and fought at Mach 3 with a 1,000-nautical-mile radius on internal fuel. It was to have a 1.2 g-limited maneuver ceiling in excess of 77,000 feet and a zoom climb ceiling of more than 100,000 feet. The Rapier was a delta wing design with a planned wingspan of 59.2 feet. The wing featured four elevons for pitch and roll control. Trim was to be provided by forward-mounted canard surfaces. The fuselage was 84.9 feet long, and the height of the aircraft was 22.1 feet from the ground to the tip of the vertical stabilizer.

The design of the F-108 continued to mature throughout its study. By 1958, the canard trimming surfaces were deleted from the forward fuselage, and the area of the delta wing was increased. The ventral fins were enlarged, but no longer extended past the upper wing surfaces. Two small ventral fins mounted on each side of the rear fuselage on the intake duct lines were added. The vertical stabilizer was given a rectangular aspect. It was found that a different rectangular intake duct with a bigger cross section was needed. The main landing gear storage had also changed. Originally, it rotated 90 degrees and folded straight ahead into bays that were in line with the intakes. The new arrangement had the right gear folding forward and the left gear folding backward at 30 degrees into the wheel wells at the center of the fuselage behind the weapons bay. Speed brakes on either side of the missile bay and thrust reverser rings on the exhaust were added for better short field landing capability.

Under normal loading and weather, the aircraft required a runway of 3,200 feet for takeoff and landing. As the design changes came into play, the weight increased by nearly 2,000 pounds although the load factor remained at 5.3. The aircraft's dimensions in the final version had changed to a span of 56.1 feet, 89 feet in length, and a height of 22.4 feet. There was one more change yet to be made. The fuselage of the F-108 was to remain the same, but the wing, which had been swept back to 58 degrees from the intake to the wingtip, now stopped about two-thirds of the way back and abruptly changed to a 32-degree sweepback to the tip and then angled back to the trailing edge.

The F-108 would be operated from 6,000-foot runways in all weather conditions. From a nominal 70,000-foot combat altitude, missile launch could have been accomplished against an air-breathing target flying at altitudes from sea level to 100,000 feet. The pulsed-Doppler radar, with its 40-inch antenna, provided target detection in excess of 100 nautical miles at all altitudes and was to be backed up by infrared search and track devices.

The F-108 was never built, but its planform appeared later in the form of the similarly shaped North American A-5 Vigilante developed for the Navy. The Vigilante holds the distinction of being the first Mach 2 aircraft to catapult from the deck of an aircraft carrier. It's not hard to look at Vigilante and imagine what the F-108 might have looked like had she been fielded.

CHAPTER 6

Just prior to the midair collision between the NASA F-104 #813 and XB-70 AV-2, the five-ship formation included the XB-70, a T-38, an F-4, and F-5, and the F-104. *Unless otherwise noted, all accident sequence photos are courtesy of AFMC/HO*

Death of a Queen

The tragic loss of the second XB-70, AV-2, in a midair collision on June 8, 1966, cast an additional pall over what was by then an already dead bomber program. It was just another nail in the coffin. Although the research program was producing valuable information and was proving the viability of a large Mach 3 aircraft, it was overshadowed by the freak accident that cost the lives of two test pilots and the loss of the more advanced of the two XB-70s.

Flying XB-70 #AV-2 that day were pilot Al White of North American and copilot Maj. Carl Cross, USAF. This was Cross's first flight in the aircraft and was an orientation ride for him. The day's primary mission of subsonic airspeed calibration runs and a supersonic boom evaluation run over ground sensors had been completed, and a photo session with the XB-70 leading a formation of General-Electric-engine-powered aircraft—F-4, F-5, T-38, and F-104—began as scheduled.

At 9:26 A.M. on June 8, 1966, 11 miles north of Barstow, California, the Valkyrie AV-2 was fatally hit. Somehow, the F-104N, tail number 813, flown by NASA pilot Joe Walker collided with the drooped right wingtip of Valkyrie AV-2. The collision sent the F-104 out of control in flames over the tails of the Valkyrie, shearing them off, then on to damage the left wing before the F-104's debris fell aft. Walker was killed instantly.

For a few seconds XB-70 AV-2 flew straight and level while White and Cross, far up front in the cockpit of the huge aircraft, listened to the calls of "midair" and tried to figure out who'd been hit. Valkyrie eventually lost the battle to stay in level flight. The conversations between the aircraft in the formation went as follows.

Close-up of NASA F-104 #813.

0918:20	AV-2:	. . . do you want to fly?
0918:24	AV-2 (White):	Turning left.
0920:02	DATA CONTROL:	Two zero seven, is tank eight feeding now? (Not on INTPH)
	AV-2 (Cross):	Al, (Also recorded on INTPH)
	AV-2 (White):	Come again, two zero seven.
	DATA CONTROL:	Ah, yes, this is Data Control. Is tank eight feeding now?
	AV-2 (Cross):	Affirmative tank eight is feeding properly now.
	DATA CONTROL:	Rog.
09:21:24	INTPH (Cross):	They must have had that Learjet full of film or they'd be out of business by now.
	AV-2 (White):	Yes—He was sitting there but he's up here now. This hole is getting smaller and smaller too.
09:22:47	#813 (Walker):	We must be helping the cumulus activity along with all this hot air.
	AV-2 (White):	Yes.
	??:	Yes.
	??:	Thank you.
09:24:48	RAPCON:	Two zero seven. Traffic. Two zero miles east of your position, orbiting Three Sisters two four zero, two seven zero.
	AV-2 (White):	Roger, Thank you.
09:25:05	AV-2 (White):	We got a contrail out there—but, I don't ah, it looks like he's higher than that.
	INTPH (Cross):	Probably—
09:25:23	#601 (Cotton):	Learjets Lear—Another four minutes the Learjet said.
	AV-2 (White):	Thanks, Joe.
09:25:40	??.	(Two carriers keyed simultaneously)
09:25:42	DATA CONTROL:	Two zero seven, the Learjet says about three more minutes.
	AV-2:	OK, Zeke.
09:26:06	RAPCON:	Two zero seven, he's off your left wing now ah, below the clouds.
	AV-2 (White):	Roger, thank you.
	RAPCON:	The B-58's speed run is now one five miles east of your position westbound three zero zero or above.
	AV-2 (White):	I have him, thank you.
09:26:26	??:	(one carrier burst followed by a longer carrier, one second maximum duration, sounding like a live microphone in an open cockpit).
09:26:28	??:	(Two or more carriers on frequency with resultant heterodynes).
	#601 (Hoag):	Mid-air, mid-air, stand by for—
	(Cotton):	You got the verticals, this is Cotton, you got the verticals—came off left and right. We're staying with ya, no sweat, now you're holding good, Al.
09:26:40	#601 (Hoag):	Joe Walker ran into him and I think he's had it.
	(Cotton):	The B-70 went upside down, it's rolling now, the left wing—
	(Hoag):	Bailout, bailout, bailout—
	(Cotton):	Bailout, bailout, bailout.
09:27:09	#601 (Cotton):	OK, the B-70 is spinning to the right—
	(Hoag):	Something came out, it looks like—
	(Cotton):	Looks like a capsule came out. It's spinning to the right, the nose is slightly down.
09:27:23	#601 (Hoag):	No chute—
	(Cotton):	. . . see no chute yet. The main gear is down, the nose gear is up.
09:27:28	#601 (Hoag):	Chute, chute, good chute.
09:27:28	#601 (Cotton):	There's a chute, there's a capsule (pause). There's one chute.
	#601 (Hoag):	B-70 wing up here to our right.
09:28:02	#601 (Cotton):	The B-70 wing is to our right. We're at fifteen thousand. The B-70 is going down. I see one chute, one capsule.
	(Hoag):	The left one.
	(Cotton):	The airplane's in a flat spin. The airplane is stable in a flat spin slightly nose down. Most of the left wing is gone. Got several pieces around us. There's a burning piece to the northwest. The airplane is flat. We're staying clear of the capsule.

Shot of formation shows F-104 closing on the XB-70's right wing. Note the contrail across the left corner, perhaps from the B-58 mentioned in the transcript of radio calls.

White and Cross finally found out who had been hit when the airplane yawed, rolled over, and began a flat spin. After some difficulty, White was able to encapsulate and eject. For some reason, Cross did not. It had been brought out that possibly he may have become disoriented, or the g-forces may not have allowed him to reach the encapsulation handle. Al White sustained life-threatening injuries, as his encapsulated ejection seat landed without the bladder inflating. His elbow was severely crushed when the clamshell door closed on it. He hung in limbo for three days before fate decided he would live. It took many months of rehabilitation to restore his injured arm to some use and to heal his internal injuries.

Carl Cross was not so lucky. He rode the flaming Valkyrie down to the desert floor and impacted at 25 Gs. Although some of the wreckage was in large pieces, most of it was pulverized. Al White had to live with the thought of leaving his copilot.

ASSIGNING BLAME

In any major test program there is always the risk that you'll lose one of your prototypes. That's why it's called flight test. There is also a chance that you will lose an aircraft in the line of duty, way past the initial flight test stage. Accidents happen. It's an unfortunate fact of life. Could the loss of the second XB-70 have been prevented? We may never know. Bureaucracy played a large part in the inquest that followed the accident. Heads rolled, blame was handed out, and changes were made;

but they were largely futile political solutions that came too late and settled nothing.

The furor that followed the crash was hard to believe. Fingers were pointed in every direction and it became obvious that scapegoat creation had begun. General Electric bore the brunt of a great deal of unfair and undeserved criticism. The photo session had been requested under the same rules, formal or informal, that had been followed dozens of times before, and the Air Force approved the routine request. After the accident, industry and Air Force heads were on the chopping block. Congress and the Administration wanted to see someone disciplined, and there were plenty of "expendable" people to choose from. Careers were destroyed and lives were ruined. After all the bloodletting, the political punishment exercise was unable to bring two dead pilots back to life or to replace a $500-million airplane.

Many questioned the competency of Joe Walker, the NASA test pilot. Walker was killed instantly when his F-104N hit the right drooped wing tip of the XB-70. It was said by a rather well-known test pilot that Walker had no business being in that formation. Was he was out of practice? Walker was a pilot with almost 5,000 hours of flight time, and over 750 hours in the F-104. No one really knows exactly what happened up there. Some assume Walker wasn't prepared to fly formation, others think he took his eyes off the Valkyrie to watch a B-58 that was coming down the corridor, or maybe he just got caught in the vortex of the XB-70 after allowing his aircraft to creep disastrously close to it. There were no records at the time

A STRUCTURAL DESCRIPTION
OF THE ACCIDENT

At 9:26 A.M. on June 8, 1966, eleven miles north of Barstow, California, the Valkyrie AV-2 was fatally hit.
The F-104N, tail number 813, flown by NASA pilot Joe Walker, collided with the drooped right wingtip of
Valkyrie AV-2. The collision sent the F-104 out of control in flames over the tails of the Valkyrie, shearing
them off, then on to damage the left wing before the F-104's debris fell aft. Walker was killed instantly.

The F-104N left wing had contacted with the XB-70 right folding wingtip leading edge, approximately 30 inches inboard of the F-104N wingtip. This cut through the upper surface of the F-104N aileron near the inboard end.

The F-104N wing moved up through the XB-70 wing and crushed and tore the steel honeycomb. There were spots of F-104N wing paint found on the lower surface face sheet of the XB-70 wing folding tip.

The F-104N left wingtip tank contacted the XB-70 leading edge forward of the hole that was cut into the XB-70 wing. The forward part of the tip tank was torn off and bent inboard and upward in relation to the F-104N. This part then separated and struck the leading edge of the F-104N vertical stabilizer. What was left of the F-104N left tip tank moved up through the XB-70 leading edge in full depth of the honeycomb panel, which rolled and moved aft, embedding several parts of the lower F-104 tip-tank-to-wing seal strip in the honeycomb at the aft end of the hole torn in the XB-70 wing.

According to the structural report contained in the accident report, the F-104N empennage hit the XB-70's right moveable vertical tail at midlevel, the upper part of the XB-70 movable vertical tail failed, twisting and bending aft.

The F-104N right side aft of the horizontal stabilizer was bent downward. There was a piece of steel honeycomb and attached face sheet from the XB-70 vertical tail, and a part of the F-104N's right stabilizer skin jammed into the aft face of the stabilizer main spar. There was also a small piece of steel honeycomb found jammed into the centerline rib of the F-104N horizontal stabilizer, and another piece was found jammed into the outboard left-hand tip section of the horizontal stabilizer. The left horizontal stabilizer was separated 20 inches outboard of the F-104N centerline. The entire F-104N empennage failed in an upward and forward motion while going left to right.

It was the upper left side of the F-104N fuselage, behind the cockpit section, that struck the leading edge of the left side of the XB-70 movable vertical, just at the hinge line, failing it from right to left, relative to the hinge point.

The F-104N cockpit and radome nose section struck the upper surface of the left-hand inboard wing of the XB-70 just outboard of the left vertical and slid across and aft on the wing surface at approximately a 30-degree angle to the elevon hinge line. Pieces of paint, and their position along the depression on the upper surface of the XB-70 wing, did match the left side of the F-104N fuselage and windshield mold line. This strike crushed and tore through the honeycomb panel of the upper cover in the XB-70 left wing.

There was a two-foot-long gash in the XB-70 left wing upper surface. It was perpendicular to the other marks and extended forward and outboard. The gash ended in a corner tear and cut in the aft inboard corner of the wing folding tip hinge inboard fairing door. The XB-70's forward inboard upper corner of the first elevon (just outboard of the wing fold hinge line) was flattened and had F-104N paint deposits on it. The upper honeycomb panel of the XB-70 left wing in the area of the fuselage station #2084 was locally crushed and torn through, starting at the wing-to-fuselage stub joint extending outboard approximately five feet.

For a few seconds after the strike, XB-70 AV-2 flew straight and level while White and Cross, far up
front in the cockpit of the huge aircraft, listened to the calls of "midair" and tried to figure out who'd been
hit. Valkyrie eventually lost the battle to stay in level flight.

Close shot of the formation seconds before the midair collision. Note the F-104's proximity to the XB-70's drooped right wingtip.

that would have indicated that Walker had recent experience with formation flying of the type that was involved in the photo-op. However, Walker had flown a T-38 in chase with an XB-70 eight times before.

No technical blame could be put on the F-104N either, even though the evidence raises suspicion. Lockheed F-104s were known to have some quirky handling problems, and the F-104N involved had some uncleared discrepancies in its logs for the June 8, 1966, flight. On May 31, 1966, there was an entry for a NAV mode of the autopilot that listed aircraft oscillations in roll plus and minus 5 degrees. On June 3, 1966, there was an entry noting only that a drag chute deployment was overdue. On June 6, 1966, there was a request for flight check of OMNI-NAV equipment, since it could not be fully checked out on the ground. On June 7, 1966, a 25-hour postflight was due. While it is unlikely that any of these unchecked items caused the crash, they are indicative of a casual attitude that may have prevailed at the time. It was noted that Joe Walker signed the exceptional release on the AFFTO Form 781, Part II, waived to make the photo-op flight. The airframe had 601 hours on it.

VORTEX THEORY

A common theory as to the cause of the crash is the so-called vortex theory. A vortex is an occurrence of whirling air that flows from the wingtip and trails behind an aircraft. It is amplified with an aircraft as heavy as the XB-70. Many believe a strong vortex caused by the XB-70's drooped wingtip may have pulled Walker's F-104 into it. Analyses indicate that there would not have been enough air pressure to cause the F-104 to lose control until it was within a few feet of the XB-70 wing. It was also noted that in previous flights with chase aircraft, the vortex effects were noted but didn't cause any effects on the chase planes. Engine wake and underbelly suction couldn't have caused the F-104 to run in the Valkyrie because of the F-104's position at the right wing of Valkyrie. Airflow did not enter into the equation until after the F-104 was already so close to the XB-70 that a collision would have occurred anyway. This was considered an "indirect contributory factor."

The F-5 pilot, John Fritz of General Electric, said that the F-104 did have some noticeable but not violent up and down and fore and aft motion on occasion during the flight, and that these were large enough to cause Fritz to "work harder" in his formation flying, but his view was

The formation about a second after the collision between the F-104 and the XB-70. The F-104 falls away in flames aft of the XB-70 while the latter momentarily remains in stable flight.

The XB-70 continues flying as the F-104 tumbles in flames farther aft.

that they "were not extreme or dangerous." Fritz also testified that prior to the impact, he had not noticed any sudden motions. It was concluded that although Joe Walker's proficiency in close formation was less than prime, it would not have resulted in the extreme motions of the F-104 that could have accounted for the accident.

The conclusion given by the accident investigation board was that the most probable cause of the XB-70 accident was inadvertent movement of the F-104 that caused it to approach a point so near the XB-70 wingtip that a collision was inevitable, and that the momentum of the collision was unstoppable.

COMMENTS ON THE ACCIDENT REPORT

One of the more interesting observations made in the official accident report came from the commentary on the film shot by the Learjet. The report stated:

"In the 35-mm movies taken from the Learjet, a streak was observed coming from the exhaust of the F-104 approximately 2 minutes and 30 seconds of film time prior to the explosion (based on 24 frames-per-second film speed). This time does not include stops made by the cameraman. The streak lasted for three frames which is 1/8 of a second elapsed time.

"The streak was first noticed on the 16-mm copy of the 35-mm master and appeared to be a streak of flame. A 35-mm copy of the master was then observed and the orange flame color appeared to lighten.

"The following possible causes of the streak were considered:

1. Discharge of carbon build-up
2. Water in fuel
3. Foreign object damage
4. Inlet ice ingestion
5. Hydraulic, lubricating oil, or fuel leak
6. Afterburner light
7. Compressor stall or surge
8. Mechanical failure within engine gas path

"The first four causes could not be eliminated as possibilities by examination of the engine or by known engine operating characteristics and remain as possible causes. Item 5 is not possible since the streak only appeared once which would require a leak that subsequently stopped. Also, a leak would not fill the complete nozzle area. Item 6, afterburner light, is not probable since the power required for the known flight conditions is approximately 90 percent and an afterburner light in this range would require large rigging error. Item 7, compressor stall, is not probable since no transient flight conditions were occurring at the time. Item 8, mechanical failure within the engine gas path, was eliminated by engine examination. It is unknown if the streaking reoccurred prior to collision."

The report concluded that neither the engine nor the aircraft fuel system had anything to do with the accident.

There are a couple of curious things about the part of the report quoted above. In the first paragraph, for example, the "streak" is reported but not described. Only in the last quoted paragraph is the streak characterized as filling the "complete nozzle area." It would seem appropriate at the outset to characterize the streak properly. There is quite a visual difference between a small streak and one that seems to emanate from the "complete nozzle area."

In the second quoted paragraph, the report states that the streak was noticed first on a 16-mm copy of the 35-mm "master" and it is implied that it was not noticed on the master itself. Then, a 35-mm copy of the master was viewed and "the orange flame color appeared to lighten." It is difficult to figure out just what the writer of the report is talking about. One is not sure just what film was viewed and the phrase "appeared to lighten" is ambiguous, to say the least. There was no mention of what actually was viewed and how the film was copied. The writer did not make the technical distinction between the original film, a master copy, or a print. It is unfortunate because it is important to the careful interpretation of the streak.

A MATTER OF TIME

There is also a time factor that applies to the USAF investigation. The accident took place on June 8, 1966. The report of the Accident Board, signed by its president, a USAF colonel, was issued on July 27, 1966. That is just 49 days! Could a really thorough investigation have been completed in such a short time?

At first examination the report appears to be thorough, but a closer review suggests that the preparation of the report was hurried. Not all the wreckage had been recovered and examined at the time the report was completed. Even in the late 1960s, FAA accident reports often took as long as a year or more to complete. The accident involved the loss of two lives, the loss of a $500-million airframe, and the destruction of half of a research "fleet" that had a program cost of nearly $1.5 billion. One might reasonably expect a more lengthy investigation. No matter how obvious the circumstances of the midair collision may have appeared, the investigation seems to have been inordinately brief.

There should have been more to this report than what had been garnered by the Air Force and the political offices involved. There was not enough time allowed to figure it out. There were new systems involved that had never been tested "under the gun" so to speak. Forty-nine days is hardly enough time for an investigation of something as complicated as the death of an XB-70 and the two who died with her. It is, however, enough to destroy a viable program and attempt to sweep it under the rug for the benefit of politics.

Continued on page 73   69

Seconds after the collision, the smaller aircraft have opened the formation and increased their distance from the XB-70, which continues flying straight and level.

XB-70 AV-2 in its last moments of stable flight.

The XB-70 has now rolled out of control more than 90 degrees to the right as it enters a flat spin.

Momentarily nose down, the XB-70 has rolled beyond 180 degrees.

Here, the XB-70 is in a gyrating flat spin, inverted, and losing fuel from the ruptured left wing.

This aerial view shows the smoke plume from the wreckage of the XB-70 after impact with the ground.

Continued from page 69

HAROLD BROWN'S MEMO

The pressure on the report writers must have been tremendous. The whole matter of the accident needed to be put in the past as quickly as possible. There was an obvious effort within the Air Force to complete the investigation and then try to forget it. This is illustrated by a memo Secretary of the Air Force Harold Brown wrote to Secretary of Defense Robert McNamara on August 12, 1966.

Brown's memo made it abundantly clear that he wasn't going to accept responsibility for the crash. He mentioned "instructions" and "procedures" that were not followed and made reference to a lack of coordination with the assistant secretary of defense for public affairs. There was no way the Air Force leadership was going to acknowledge the photographic mission as standard procedure. The memo, however, never spelled out which regulations were violated. Nothing was said about why such photo missions had been taking place openly for years without comment from Air Force leadership.

Brown said that under established procedures, requests for Air Force assistance in the production of commercial films required approval at a high level. He indicated that this procedures list included not only theatrical motion pictures, but also industrial motion pictures of advertising value. The director of information for the Air Force was supposed to be the sole authority.

In reality, the director of information was supposed to coordinate with the assistant secretary of defense (public affairs). The assistant secretary of defense (public affairs) had the primary responsibility for relations with industry, so questions on the extent of cooperation would be referred to him. In view of Secretary of Defense McNamara's desire to oversee all of the press and PR releases for all the services including NASA, this practice would not seem unusual.

There were other directives that prohibited flights of USAF aircraft not in the direct interest of government business. Air Force participation in contractor-sponsored special events was restricted and was not to be used to support commercial advertising, publicity, or promotional activities. OSD approval was required on all aerial reviews not otherwise authorized.

Brown continued in the memo to say that the XB-70 flight in question never had such approval, at least not for the General Electric part of the flight. Brown concluded that the Air Force officer who assisted General Electric with this exercise used poor judgment, and that this officer's superior was also to blame because he didn't exercise good judgment in his duties. There were also two other Air Force officers cited: "an Air Force information officer and an official at the next higher level of the XB-70 program, both of whom were aware of the formation flight but failed to do anything about it." Brown finished his prologue with a statement that there were going to be further measures taken to ensure that the lessons of this accident were learned.

In this report there was a review made of all the contracts held with North American Aviation and General Electric. Of course, it showed that there were no provisions made for photography for nongovernmental purposes. They were not authorized or required. This photographic mission was therefore ". . . outside the terms of these contracts and could not properly have been undertaken unless approved in accordance with the procedures on pictorial and industrial relations activities noted at the outset." This statement says that this was an illegal flight sanctioned by the Air Force, which said that its officers acted incorrectly.

THE MAKINGS OF AN "ILLEGAL" FLIGHT

General Electric started the ball rolling for the photomission sometime in mid-May of 1966, when its chief test pilot John Fritz approached a senior representative of North American at the Edwards AFB Flight Test Center. Fritz was asked by General Electric to see whether it would be possible to arrange for in-flight photos of the XB-70 in formation with other supersonic aircraft using General Electric engines. The North American representative said it might be worked out, depending on the availability of the XB-70.

John Fritz then contacted Colonel Joe Cotton, who was the test director for the XB-70 program. Colonel Cotton agreed to the inclusion of the photo session at the end of a test flight as long as it did not interfere and if large demands were not made on the Air Force Flight Test Center. Colonel Cotton had permitted North American to take in-flight photos of the Sabreliner and the XB-70 on a noninterference basis. He felt consideration should be given to General Electric's request. He also felt that General Electric responded positively to the flight test program.

On June 2, 1966, Colonel Cotton requested and received approval for the flight from his supervisor, Colonel Cate, deputy for Systems Test, AFFTC. The following is Colonel Cotton's testimony:

"The main thing here, when I realized we were going to have a formation, was I didn't think it was appropriate to see a five- or six-ship formation someplace without folks here at home knowing it. I felt it was important to discuss it with the boss and tell him it was a request for General Electric and to point out that we had done it before, and see what he thought about it and get his guidance on it. . . ."

There was no further approval sought or secured, except for the briefing of Colonel Cate by Colonel Cotton on the details. Once a decision had been reached, John Fritz started the arrangements for the following aircraft to participate in the flight:

A close-up of XB-70's wing wreckage.

Al White's clamshell escape capsule is shown resting on the desert floor.

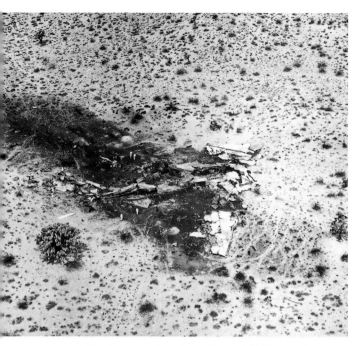

This is an aerial view of the XB-70 wreckage where it impacted on the floor of the desert.

Wreckage of Maj. Carl Cross' clamshell ejection capsule on the desert floor.

(1) XB-70.

(2) AFFTC T-38. It was scheduled to participate in the flight as a chase aircraft. There were always chase planes on any XB-70 flight.

(3) F-104N supplied by NASA. It was made available for the photo mission by Joe Walker who was the chief research pilot for NASA at Edwards. The request for this aircraft by John Fritz was backed by Colonel Cotton even though it was not needed for chase flight. The flight was scheduled by Joe Walker as a chase operation, which was under his authority at NASA (although his superiors did not know of the photo mission).

(4) Navy F-4 Phantom from Pt. Mugu Naval Air Station, California. This was secured by John Fritz with Commander Jerome Skyrud, head of Air-to-Air Weapons branch, Naval Missile Center. It was approved by the operations coordination officer as a routine training flight in support of what was assumed to be an approved Air Force mission.

(5) F-5. Air Force-owned, but bailed to General Electric under unrelated engine component improvement programs. In the technical sense there was a requirement that all flights of bailed aircraft must be approved. This was complied with, but in fact the F-5 did not perform the engine airstart evaluations (the "official" reason for its inclusion) as stated by John Fritz in the documentation for this flight.

It was also noted that John Fritz attempted to arrange for an Air Force B-58, but was unsuccessful. He also unsuccessfully tried to arrange for Air Force photo coverage.

A Learjet was contracted by General Electric to photograph the formation.

Brown goes on in the report to state that the XB-70 had a reason to be in the air along with the T-38 aside from the photo session. The F-104N was also considered to be of importance since Joe Walker had flown chase on the XB-70 eight times and was training to be a XB-70 pilot. His first familiarization flight was slated for June 10. The rest of the aircraft involved, according to Brown, lacked sufficient reason to be involved in the photographic mission.

The photo session was officially added to the research flight on June 2, 1966. It was tagged to the end of an airspeed calibration run and a familiarization flight for Major Carl Cross. On June 7, a third objective was added to the list: a sonic boom run for the SST program. In the official paperwork for preflight reports, only these three missions were mentioned.

A preflight briefing was held on June 7. North American handled the technical end of the flight while John Fritz handled the photographic session. A "loose V" formation that was going to be led by the XB-70 was proposed rather than a close formation. The F-104 was assigned the inboard position and flown by Joe Walker from NASA. This was off the right wing of the XB-70. Commander Skyrud in the F-4 was given the inboard position on the left side. John Fritz was assigned the right outboard position, and Captain Pete Hoag, in the Air Force T-38, was in the left outboard position, with Colonel Cotton in the rear seat. The Learjet was out of the formation. There were no specific separation distances discussed and

Close-up of F-104 ejection seat wreckage.

no formation commander assigned, although Colonel Cotton figured himself to be in charge.

Three of the pilots from the flight were not present at the briefing: Al White, who assumed command as XB-70 pilot on June 7 when the original pilot had to drop out for another flight; Commander Skyrud, who kept in contact with John Fritz via telephone; and H. Clay Lacy, who was the Learjet pilot briefed by John Fritz before takeoff on June 8. On the Learjet, there was a General Electric test pilot who was familiar with Edwards AFB procedures and had attended the preflight briefing.

It should be noted that a Mr. John McCollum was also involved. He was the director of research vehicles for the aeronautical systems division and served as the XB-70 system program director. At the time, he was visiting Edwards AFB to discuss the next phase of the XB-70 test program with the Test Center, NASA, and contractor personnel. On June 7, he helped in the scheduling of the sonic boom run and, on invitation, he attended the preflight briefing. He was the highest-ranking Air Force official at the briefing and he knew about the photographic mission. Since he did not object to this photo session, he seems to have given it his unexpressed consent. If he did object, the mission would not have been able to go on, as it was within his jurisdiction to take the XB-70 out of the flight.

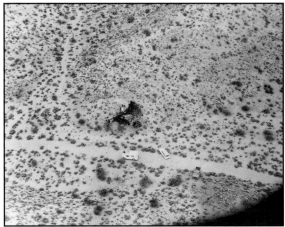

An aerial view of the F-104 crash site.

THE FLIGHT ACCORDING TO THE MEMO

XB-70 AV-2 took off at approximately 7:15 A.M. to run the airspeed calibration tests. There was the ever present chase aircraft following her, this time a T-38. When the XB-70 started her climb for a sonic boom run, the T-38 had to land to refuel; another T-38 in the area checked the XB-70 to make sure that the cooling doors were closed. The sonic boom run was completed by 8:30 A.M. and it appears that

Close-up view of wreckage of the F-104's forward section on the desert floor.

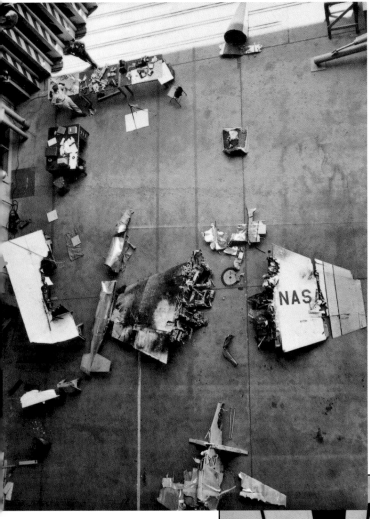

the rendezvous portion of the mission was completed at about 8:45 A.M. There were clouds in the area that made a change in altitude necessary—from the prescribed 20,000 feet to 25,000 feet. Location and direction were also changed from north-south to east-west, the latter resulting in a much shorter flight path. The XB-70 flew in a left-hand race track pattern at 300 knots IAS, with the Learjet following 500 feet or more from the formation, to the left and slightly behind. No problems were reported with the formation and it continued on its way to destiny for about 40 minutes.

The report says that at around 9:00 A.M., an Air Force photo aircraft on a return from another mission had 100 feet of unexpended film. That flight asked for and received permission to film the formation in progress. At 9:15 A.M., the Learjet was questioned about additional time, since the already-planned-for 30 minutes had elapsed. The Learjet requested an additional 10-15 minutes. Just before 9:26 A.M. the Learjet called in and stated that another three minutes would meet their requirements.

At 9:26 A.M., the NASA F-104 collided with the XB-70. The first contact was with the left horizontal stabilizer and the canted right wingtip of the XB-70. The F-104 then pitched up, rolled to the left, and hit the right leading edge of the XB-70's wing. The F-104 continued its roll inverted into the XB-70's top right vertical stabilizer and took the top off the left vertical stabilizer. The F-104 was cut just aft of the cockpit. The nose of the F-104 hit the XB-70's left wing, and the fuselage of the F-104 went

Overhead view of F-104 wreckage laid out on the floor of a hangar.

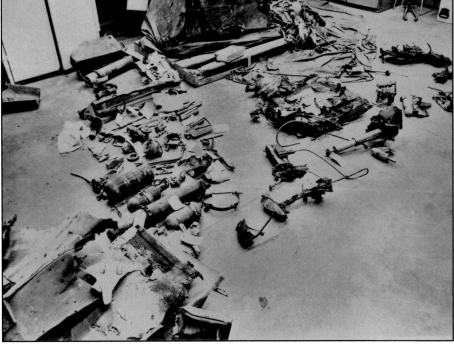

Layout in the hangar of XB-70 clamshell ejection seat.

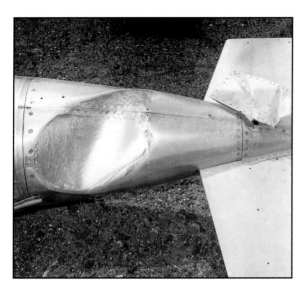

Close-up showing damage to F-104 wingtip tank.

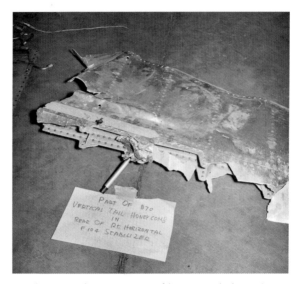

This view shows a piece of honeycomb from the XB-70's vertical tail imbedded in the right rear section of the F-104's horizontal stabilizer.

streaking aft in flames. The XB-70 continued to hold her own for a few seconds, then lost her maneuverability. The left wing failed, and the second XB-70 entered Valhalla one minute and 52 seconds after the collision.

Harold Brown's summary of the XB-70 disaster showed just how hurriedly this report was put together, presumably so that it could be swept under the rug. Nothing could have pleased Mr. McNamara more. Not only was there resistance to finding out the real reasons the accident happened, but Brown also seemed insistent that General Electric was to be blamed without a doubt. The apparent attitude was that none of this would have happened if General Electric hadn't asked for the photo flight. Colonel Cotton would be assigned the blame for not refusing the request and overriding North American Aviation's reluctance to cooperate. Colonel Cate would take the blame for his limited view of his approval authority (which had never been challenged before in other photo-op issues). And, of course, Mr. McCollum would be blamed for not stopping the flight altogether. No one ever questioned why this practice had occurred so many times before without objections.

According to Brown, all those people and companies were working in complete "ignorance of the prescribed procedures, rather than with intent to violate them." Mr. Brown also questioned the judgment of the people who made this whole episode possible: the Air Force, the civilian contractors and, of course, the General Electric Company. Conveniently not mentioned was the office of the assistant secretary of defense (public affairs), apparently because they had not been informed of the flight.

Brown strongly implied that this accident would never have happened at something as legitimate as an

F-104 left wingtip tank. Close-up of what is believed to be the point of initial contact with the XB-70.

"Armed Forces Day event." Such a flight would have required the approval of the Air Force director of information, and the assistant secretary of defense (public affairs). He cited an instance where merely for the XB-70 to appear an air show at Carswell AFB, Texas, the request had reached the highest level of the Air Force chief of staff and the secretary of the Air Force, and then the appearance was limited to a static display. Why it would take the approval of the Air Force chief of staff to approve a static display, but a formation flight could be approved by a secretary of

XB-70 right wingtip droop section leading edge showing imbedded fairing strip from the F-104 left wingtip tank. The pen at the right bottom corner of the sign indicates the area.

XB-70 right wing droop section leading edge. Note upward deformation of the edge strip.

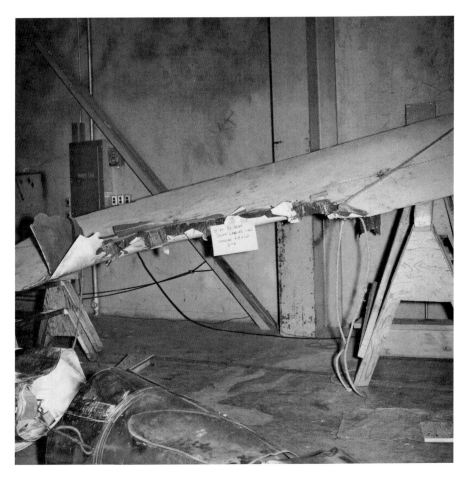

Leading edge of the XB-70's drooping right wingtip section showing the 6x2-foot missing section.

defense public affairs officer and an Air Force public affairs officer, defies understanding.

As always in disasters of this magnitude, disciplinary actions were taken. Colonel Cate was relieved of duty as deputy for systems tests, given a written reprimand, and assigned other duties. Colonel Cotton, Mr. McCollum, and Colonel Smith were also given written reprimands. But did this breakdown in communications and the reprimands bring back two dead pilots, a $500-million aircraft, and a $1.5-billion program with extensive research capabilities? The answer is no. It solved nothing. It didn't even analyze the reasons why the F-104 rolled into the XB-70. There was only speculation about the cause. It left a pilot tainted with the possibility of being unprepared to fly in that formation. It left open to question the reliability of the XB-70 in handling: could she just be too much aircraft to handle? It left open the question of the death of a pilot in an escape system that *almost* worked perfectly, but didn't.

The recommendations of the investigation board to prevent any such occurrence in the future were passed on. First, the importance of the operational procedures was emphasized. Test directors had to have a certain amount of leeway to perform their duties, but not so much that higher-ups could not ensure policy compliance. The escape system was to be modified to make sure high g-forces wouldn't hinder escape.

And, finally, formation flying was to reach a new level of standards, especially with mixed aircraft types in the formation, such as in chase operations. So much for pinning the blame.

Harold Brown's report did offer hypotheses as to the cause of the accident:

A. Air turbulence causing motion of one of the aircraft.
B. Mechanical malfunction on one of the aircraft.
C. Physiological problems of one of the crew.
D. Distraction of the F-104 pilot.
E. Aerodynamic effects on the F-104 due to airflow near the XB-70.
F. F-104 pilot formation proficiency.
G. Inadvertent movement of the F-104 into the XB-70 not perceptible to the pilot.

A. Air turbulence—the XB-70 telemetered traces indicated little or no acceleration about any airplane axis, conclusively ruling out any abrupt motion of the XB-70 in pitch, roll, or yaw. John Fritz, the F-5 pilot who was flying in a position close to the F-104, which was between his aircraft and the XB-70, stated that there was no turbulence during this period, nor was it reported by other members of the formation. Since turbulence is not normally confined to an area small enough to affect single aircraft within a

Air Force Secretary Harold Brown.

flight . . . without being felt by any other member of the flight, turbulence can be discounted as a contributory factor in the collision.

B. Malfunction of the XB-70 is ruled out. Although a malfunction in the F-104 cannot be completely eliminated from consideration, the probability of this being a causative factor is very remote.

C. The XB-70 pilot indicated no physiological problem to himself either in testimony or statement. As he was flying the aircraft at impact, physiological problems in the XB-70 crew can be eliminated in causative considerations.

D. The postmortem examination of Mr. Walker indicates little or no likelihood of pre-collision coronary problems. Due to the condition of the body, the determination of whether precollision dysbarism or hypoxia existed cannot be made with certainty.

E. No other pilot in the formation noticed any abrupt or unusual movement of the F-104 or Mr. Walker prior to the initial collision. Although this supports to a large extent the possibility that Mr. Walker was not suffering physiological problems, it also is not totally conclusive. Even slight hypoxia could result in loss of judgment on the part of the pilot and a gradual movement of the F-104 into the XB-70 that might not be sensed by him.

F. Mr. Walker was distracted from what he was doing. One possible reason was the B-58 sonic boom run approaching from the opposite direction and above the formation. This was reported by RAPCON about 16 seconds prior to the collision.

G. Al White reported that he had the B-58 in sight, and the memo conjectures that Joe Walker took his eyes off the "road," which is also cited as "highly unlikely" with someone of his experience. There were other more remote possibilities such as something happening inside the cockpit that might have distracted Walker.

LIVES AT STAKE

Joe Walker lost his life when the left vertical stabilizer of the XB-70 severed the F-104 behind the cockpit or when the forward area of the F-104 struck the left wing of the XB-70. There was no time to eject. The elapsed time of the impact was something like 2.8 seconds. Of course, g-forces came into play, and there was no escape.

Carl Cross lost his life when he was unable to eject in the escape capsule. There are two ways that the ejection could have been initiated:

A. The clamshell doors could have been closed manually after the seat was moved aft manually. This couldn't have been done in the presence of the g-forces that the aircraft was already experiencing.

B. The second way, which was used on this day, was "ballistic encapsulation." The pilot would have raised one or both of the arm rests and the gas pressure from charges would have moved the seat back and closed the clamshell door. When either armrest is raised, the trigger is exposed. Squeezing the trigger completed the ejection sequence. If there were forward forces greater than the gas charges could compensate for, or beyond the safety burst mechanism, the gas charge would have been lost without seat retraction and escape would have been impossible. After ejection, certain sequences would have occurred automatically. This included chute deployment and pressurization of a gas-filled "attenuation bag" for reducing the landing shock. There was redundancy inside the capsule just in case some of the automatic sequences failed.

In Al White's testimony, he reported that he "seemed for a period of time to be unable to move in the capsule due to the loads throwing him forward and to the left, even after he heard the call, Bail out! Bail out! Bail out!" He finally pulled the right handle of his escape capsule and encapsulated ballistically. He failed to keep his right elbow inside the capsule and it became wedged in the clamshell door. He was able to free his arm and eject. He could not contact or help Carl Cross because of his own difficulty.

His chute finally opened and White closed the door of the capsule manually. He lost the emergency checklist during ejection and was aware that the bladder on the underside of the capsule, which was supposed to cushion the landing, was not inflated, but he could not recall where the inflation switch was. Although Harold Brown's memo says that Al White sustained minor injuries, he in fact sustained major internal damage.

Carl Cross's failure to escape was not because of lack of training, even though this was his first flight. Lifting armrests and squeezing triggers was a common practice in Air Force aircraft in which Carl Cross had much experience.

Carl Cross could not eject. The possibilities given in the memo were:
A. Failure to follow proper ejection procedures.
B. Escape system failure.
C. Forces beyond the system capability due to the XB-70 motions.
D. Major Cross was burned or injured during White's ejection.
E. Incapacitation from injury due to the violence of the XB-70 motion.
F. Failure to remove a safety pin prior to flight.

The consensus was that Carl Cross was incapacitated by the g-forces affecting him as the XB-70 began its flat, spiral dive to the floor of the desert, and he could not manually eject. Al White in his testimony said, "For the next few seconds I seemed unable to move in the capsule; the loads being somewhat oscillatory, throwing us forward and to the left. During this period of time I tried to talk, thinking that I had a hot mike; but I could only hear myself grunting under the excitement and extreme force that seemed to be exerted on us and throwing us forward and to the left. While I was trying to free my arm, I did observe Major Cross's head bobbing in the right-hand capsule. . . . I was aware that the main force was throwing me forward at this time. . . ."

Perhaps Carl Cross became incapacitated by some sort of injury when Al White ejected from the XB-70; possibly by the ejection rocket blast. Or he could have been knocked out by violent forces in the falling airplane, even though he was wearing a seat harness and was helmeted. There was no conclusive reason given for his death, only supposition to the cause. A possibility of ejection system failure was also noted by the board of inquiry, but proved once again inconclusive.

It could have been a case of "bad timing" with Al White's ejection, but the fact that Carl Cross was not encapsulated when Al White ejected and that White could see Cross' "head bobbing," leads to the conclusion that he might have already been unconscious.

CHAPTER 7

A-12 Blackbird resting at Blackbird Park, California. *Courtesy Kirk Davenport*

The Blackbird Factor

Some believe that Lockheed and its A-12, YF-12, and SR-71 Blackbirds were responsible for the demise of the XB-70 Valkyrie. They believe the B-70 program was canceled because of the pressure Lockheed—specifically Kelly Johnson, head of Lockheed's Advanced Development Projects, a.k.a. the Skunk Works—placed on the Oval Office. This is far from what actually happened. The Blackbirds, while being Mach 3 capable, were so totally different from the XB-70 that they were not in competition with each other. In fact, one program aided the other when it came to cutting-edge technology. North American and Lockheed never intended to compete, but the politicians didn't quite see it that way.

Kelly Johnson was asked if the A-12 could be transformed into an intercontinental bomber, or at least some form of weapons delivery platform. The answer was yes, but Lockheed would have to address not only the relatively short range of the A-12, but its limited load-carrying capability if it were to be made into a truly capable intercontinental bomber. Richard Bissell, who was then in charge of the CIA, informed Kennedy that an A-12 transformation might be possible. Kennedy asked him, "Could Kelly Johnson convert the spy plane into a long-range bomber?" Bissell responded that the conversion was exactly what Kelly Johnson had planned to do. "Then why do we need the B-70 program?" Kennedy asked. Bissell suggested that the president ask the question of General LeMay.

It was not Kelly Johnson and the Skunk Works that proposed the demise of the B-70, it was Bissell. It appears to have come down to a political move on the part of the CIA to further advance its own status by attaching itself to the glory of the Skunk Works. Kelly Johnson, however, maintains that the final cancellation of the B-70 program was not his idea but that of Richard Bissell.

Interestingly enough, Bissell soon afterward found himself out of power because of his part in the ill-fated Bay of Pigs invasion. Not much later, Kelly Johnson, feeling pressure from Robert McNamara, began to harbor some cancellation concerns of his own. Johnson was afraid that with Bissell out of power, McNamara, in a cost-cutting frenzy, would cancel the very expensive and very secret Blackbird program.

It is important to emphasize that the A-12 Blackbird, and her sisters the YF-12 and the SR-71, were not designed to perform the same functions as the B-70, despite attempts by the Air Force and others to cast the two in the same mold. There were major differences in their construction and operations, as well as their performance. The B-70 was designed as a strategic bomber. It was never intended to be stealthy. It was not designed for reconnaissance work (although the Air

A HELPING HAND:
FROM KELLY JOHNSON'S LOG

The Blackbird and XB-70 programs aided each other when it came to cutting-edge technology. In his log, Kelly Johnson wrote of his desires to help the struggling B-70 program:

MARCH 12, 1962

"It appears that our problem with Viton shows that the material planned for the B-70 is no good, either. Sent information and a can of our sealant to Wright Field for use by [General Fred] Ascani [B-70 Program Director] to help the B-70."

DECEMBER 5, 1962

". . . We are helping the B-70 all we can, because they are in real trouble on tank sealing and wiring and other things. I wrote General Ascani a letter promising our assistance, which we have given verbally many times in the past."

AUGUST 14, 1964

"Fred Rall of ASD and Ed Dawson of North American came here to discuss hydraulic problems on the B-70. I am amazed to find they built no hydraulic mock-up whatsoever and they are into troubles that we solved in 1961. Incidentally, I showed Dawson a letter I had written to General Ascani in 1961, pointing out these problems."

Force tried to sell the reconnaissance role to Congress at one point in an attempt to save the program). It was never intended to be anything but a high-altitude, intercontinental strategic bomber with Mach 3 capability. These focused goals were not a weakness. The XB-70 was a formidable machine by anyone's measure.

Both programs had difficulty building aircraft out of materials that could withstand the high temperatures associated with high-speed flight. At 80,000-feet altitude, the ambient air temperature was around minus 60-degrees Fahrenheit, but at 2,000 miles per hour the skin temperature would approach 600-degrees Fahrenheit. Each program found a different solution to this problem. Development of the XB-70 brought about the first extensive use of stainless steel honeycomb, but only after new autoclaves were designed to support the large sizes required. A new brazing technique had to be developed to make sure that the "weld" would not be compromised by vibration or heat. Some of the constraints included wearing special gloves so that natural oils from the workers' fingers would not interfere with the integrity of the weld. The A-12 was having similar problems with its exotic titanium skin. Although it was as strong as stainless steel, titanium was a largely untried material, particularly in the quantities used in the A-12.

Both Lockheed and North American made use of heat sink technology to handle some of the airframe heat loads and in both cases the primary onboard heat sink was fuel. In the A-12, the airframe was largely uninsulated, and though it used heat-resistant titanium, some of the heat was absorbed by the fuel. Fuel also was actually used as a hydraulic fluid for the engine controls. The cockpit was pressurized, but not well insulated, so the pilot had to wear a pressure suit at all times for temperature protection as well as protection against sudden depressurization.

The XB-70 was a much larger airplane and carried an enormous fuel load, which made for a very suitable heat sink. In addition, the XB-70 was insulated, aided further by the honeycomb skin. The crew cabin could be kept at a relatively comfortable temperature, and the larger volume of pressurized space within the aircraft meant that any depressurization would be more gradual. The crew of the B-70 could operate in a "shirtsleeve" environment.

Weight and payload performance differed greatly between the Blackbirds and the Valkyrie. The B-70 was designed to carry a heavy, destructive payload the Blackbirds could never match. The extra payload ability of the B-70 was also utilized for fuel. The B-70 had a longer unrefueled range than the Blackbirds, and the B-70 could take off with a full fuel load. The Blackbirds had to refuel shortly after takeoff to enable them to reach operational speed and

CIA Article #122, the flight test vehicle for the A-12 Blackbird, looking even more alien aboard the USS *Intrepid* Sea-Air-Space Museum. *Photo by author*

A-12 #121 on its maiden flight. The mountains in the background were air-brushed out in a recent reproduction of this same photo. *AFMC/HO*

altitude. Weight was always a problem for the Blackbirds, and they wrestled with it on a continuing basis.

There were also operational differences between the two aircraft. There was no quick turnaround system developed for the A-12. It took a minimum of three hours of preflight to get the A-12 into the air. It also required a special start cart with twin Buick auto racing engines to get the J-58 engines up to the 3,000 rpm needed to start.

The B-70 would be able to start up via one engine and an alert pod, which was similar to a start cart but physically attached to the engine bay. For a combat operational B-70 on alert status, it was supposed to take no more than two minutes from startup to runway. From a cold start it would take only 20 minutes. The quick start feature was never tested in the two XB-70s because they were not intended to be combat operational aircraft, but the procedures were in place for the production model.

Aircraft operations aside, program operations were different as well. The A-12 was highly classified and the B-70 was not. Publicity for the two programs was a double-edged sword and they each handled it in their own way. Publicity was not a problem for the B-70 program. The futuristic bomber was in the media's spotlight, and both the Air Force and North American basked in it, particularly early on in the program. The B-70 received considerable attention in the national news, aviation magazines, and other publications. While some aspects of it were classified, it was not a "black" program, so money was saved by not keeping it secret. On the other hand, lack of secrecy meant that the B-70 program was fair game for budget-cutting politicians. Conversely, the Blackbirds had to live in deep secrecy. They lost out on the benefit of the media, but avoided budget cuts, as most politicians did not know they existed.

The XB-70 and the A-12 evolved around the same time, but on different ends of the "flight line." The B-70 was open to the observations and opinions of all while the A-12 was wrapped in the dark world of the CIA. Many of their systems were entirely different. However, one did rely on the other even if it was for just a fuel pump or a technological concept. They were not the enemies that many tried to make them out to be.

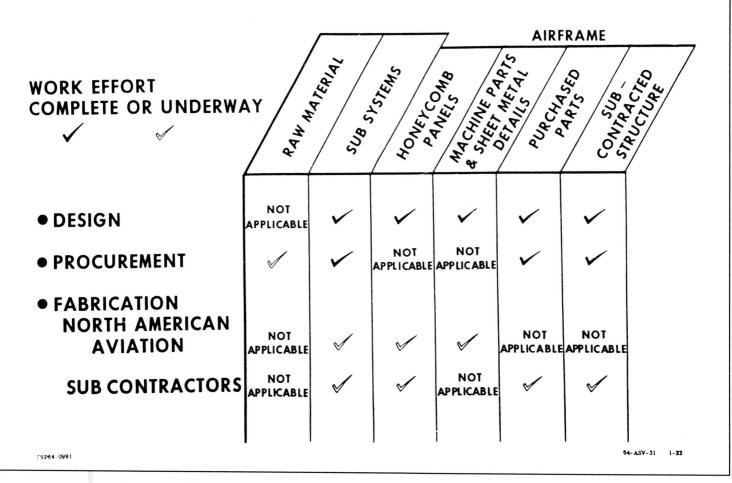

CHAPTER 8

AIR VEHICLE NO.3

WORK EFFORT
COMPLETE OR UNDERWAY ✓ ✓

AIRFRAME

	RAW MATERIAL	SUB SYSTEMS	HONEYCOMB PANELS	MACHINE PARTS & SHEET METAL DETAILS	PURCHASED PARTS	SUB-CONTRACTED STRUCTURE
● DESIGN	NOT APPLICABLE	✓	✓	✓	✓	✓
● PROCUREMENT	✓	✓	NOT APPLICABLE	NOT APPLICABLE	✓	✓
● FABRICATION NORTH AMERICAN AVIATION	NOT APPLICABLE	✓	✓	✓	NOT APPLICABLE	NOT APPLICABLE
SUB CONTRACTORS	NOT APPLICABLE	✓	✓	NOT APPLICABLE	✓	✓

FSP64-0991

64-ASV-31   1-22

Program study breakdown of progress on AV-3 shows that work was just about halfway completed before cancellation. *AFMC/HO*

The Elusive Third Valkyrie

Not very much has been written about AV-3, the third Valkyrie. AV-3 was to carry tail number #20208, but she was canceled on February 15, 1964, and never completed. Only a few people really knew that she was to be very different from the other two Valkyries. The Air Force had plans for her because she was the bomber that they had been hoping for.

The design for AV-3 was completed on October 31, 1963. Because her sisters had paved the way, a lot of the technical problems had already been worked out. Previous problems such as the complicated brazing techniques, the redesign of the honeycomb panels for fabrication, and the elimination of assembly problems had already been solved.

It wasn't long before the construction of AV-3 was under way. The procurement process for her raw materials was finished. The aircraft required 24,452 square feet of honeycomb core PH15-7, sheet metal quoted at 157,846 pounds, and 26,403 feet of linear extrusions. The fabrication processes on the subsystems and the subcontracted structure were all on schedule—all except for the "key" honeycomb panels needed for the biggest part of the assembly operation. The honeycomb panel design was complete, but the fabrication of the honeycomb panels was still underway. By January 24, 1964, the Bombing and Navigation (Bomb/Nav) systems developed by IBM—and the Doppler radar—had passed acceptance tests. Radar sighting equipment had passed acceptance tests at General Electric and was delivered on time. The integration tests at IBM were all on schedule. The digital computer had completed its functional test with the Doppler radar.

ALTERNATE PLANS

During the construction of the third Valkyrie, the Air Force managers were fighting to save the program. They had devised seven alternate plans, each one trying to save something of AV-3, or for that matter, trying to salvage everything possible of the entire program. All the alternatives were based on a pared-to-the-bone proposal, with hopes of building three air vehicles and flying two of them. The flight test program was to be just extensive enough to prove the range of the envelope, including flight work at Mach 3.

Supporters hoped the seven programs would yield a gold mine of information on high-performance vehicles, including data on speed, payload, altitude, and duration of flights at high speed. The SST program testing (funded by NASA), was a big selling point for NASA, the Air Force, and congressional interests and was being relied on to reverse the lagging

MAJOR SYSTEM STATUS

SUBSYSTEM	HARDWARE DELIVERY STATUS			AIRWORTHINESS STATUS
	(AIR VEHICLE NO. 1)	(AIR VEHICLE NO. 2)	(AIR VEHICLE NO. 3)	
WING FOLD ACTUATOR	COMPLETE	COMPLETE	JULY '64	COMPLETE
ENVIRONMENTAL CONTROL SYSTEM	COMPLETE	COMPLETE	JUNE '64	COMPLETE
CENTRAL AIR DATA SYSTEM	COMPLETE	COMPLETE	COMPLETE	COMPLETE
AUXILIARY GYRO PLATFORM SYSTEM	COMPLETE	COMPLETE	COMPLETE	COMPLETE
FUEL BOOST AND TRANSFER PUMPS	COMPLETE	COMPLETE	SEPT '64	COMPLETE
ENGINE EXTRACTION AIR DUCTING SYSTEM	COMPLETE	COMPLETE	MAR '64	COMPLETE
LANDING GEAR	COMPLETE	COMPLETE	MAY '64	COMPLETE
SECONDARY POWER GENERATING SYSTEM	COMPLETE	COMPLETE	MAY '64	COMPLETE
FLIGHT AUGMENTATION CONTROL SYSTEM	COMPLETE	MAR '64	JUN '64	COMPLETE
FUEL INERTING SYSTEM	COMPLETE	COMPLETE	JULY '64	COMPLETE
FUEL MANAGEMENT SYSTEM	COMPLETE	COMPLETE	JUN '64	COMPLETE
AIR INDUCTION CONTROL SYSTEM	JAN '64	MAR '64	JUN '64	COMPLETE

TSP64-0097   64-ASV-31   1-28

This chart shows the various levels of hardware delivery for each of the three Valkyries. *AFMC/HO*

public interest in an American-built SST. Other programs on the table, such as the AMPSS (Advanced Manned Precision Strike System), which later became the B-1 bomber; the SRAM (Short-Range Attack Missile); the multisensor evaluation program (Program 679A); and the advanced air-to-surface missiles (ADO-51) helped cloud the issue further.

The proposals concluded that all three XB-70s should be completed in the country's national interest. Supporters hoped that the program could stay under the $1.5-billion mark and agreed that the potential of the XB-70 program was enormous.

AIR VEHICLE #3

AV-3 was to be different from the other two Valkyries. She was to carry a four-man crew, two pilots and two observers, in what later would have been Bomb/Nav Officer and Defensive Systems Officer. The radome was able to support 130 cubic feet of equipment for 1,000 pounds of such things as star trackers, antennas, and so on. New requirements for the equipment bay caused it to grow to 300 cubic feet to accommodate 12,000 pounds of new sophisticated "toys." The weapons bay was enlarged to 1,200 cubic feet and could hold 25,000 pounds of ordnance. The structural difference between

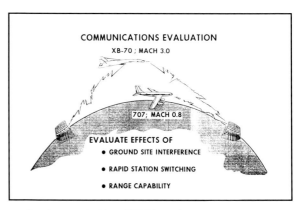

An almost primitive JSTARS configuration was considered for the third Valkyrie. Some of it was connected with the RSB (Reconnaissance-Strike Bomber) proposal that was coming up. *AFMC/HO*

the other two Valkyries and AV-3 would have been seen in the lower fuselage. The third Valkyrie's lower fuselage was not compatible with the other two, so cannibalization to support it would not have been possible. The structure was changed to accommodate a new environmental control system and the associated ducting and plumbing needed for a four-man crew compartment and for cooling the electronic equipment.

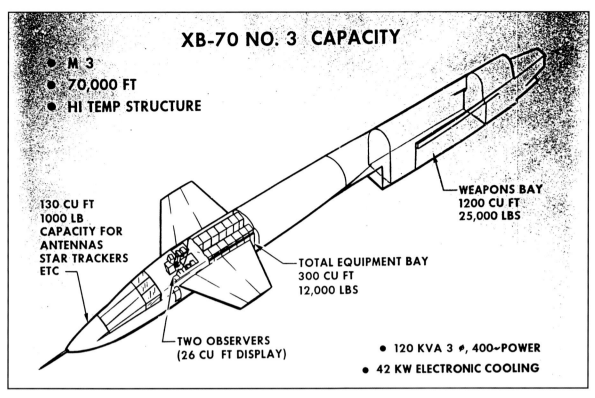

XB-70 NO. 3 CAPACITY

- M 3
- 70,000 FT
- HI TEMP STRUCTURE

130 CU FT
1000 LB
CAPACITY FOR
ANTENNAS
STAR TRACKERS
ETC

TWO OBSERVERS
(26 CU FT DISPLAY)

TOTAL EQUIPMENT BAY
300 CU FT
12,000 LBS

WEAPONS BAY
1200 CU FT
25,000 LBS

- 120 KVA 3 ∅, 400∼POWER
- 42 KW ELECTRONIC COOLING

Capacity differences between AV-3, AV-1, and AV-2 are illustrated in this drawing. Note the positioning of two additional crew members forward of the equipment bay location. *AFMC/HO*

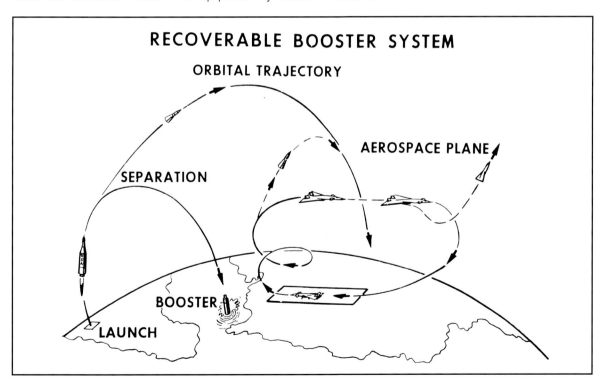

RECOVERABLE BOOSTER SYSTEM

ORBITAL TRAJECTORY

SEPARATION

AEROSPACE PLANE

BOOSTER

LAUNCH

The proposed recoverable booster system would permit the attainment of an orbital trajectory. *AFMC/HO*

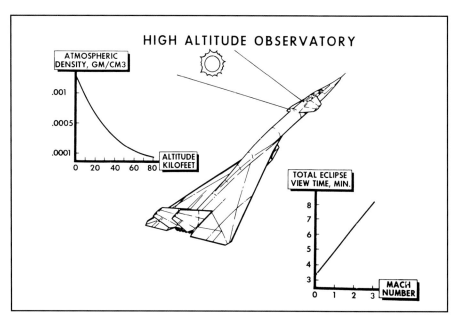

HIGH ALTITUDE OBSERVATORY

Part of the "wish list" was the concept of a high-altitude observatory, which would provide better access to astronomical phenomena than a ground-based observatory. For example, an XB-70-based observatory would be able to follow a solar eclipse along its earthly path rather than be limited by observations from a single point on the ground. *AFMC/HO*

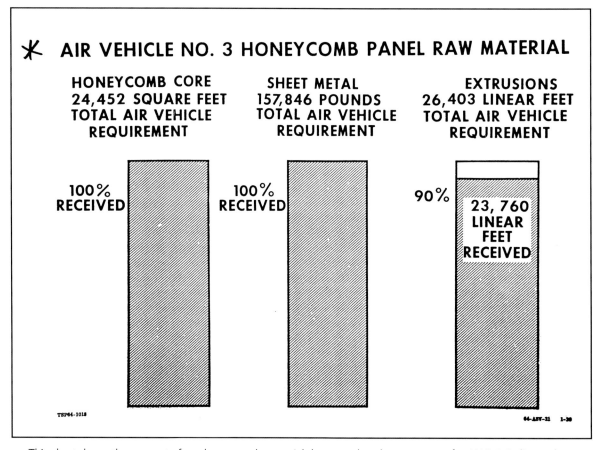

This chart shows the amount of raw honeycomb material that was already on contract for AV-3. It indicates how much of the third XB-70 was already accounted for and waiting to be assembled. *AFMC/HO*

There was another interesting fact concerning the third Valkyrie. Because of the shape of the engine inlet ducts, the Valkyrie was considered to be a prime candidate for evaluating the performance of RAM (radar absorbent material) coatings placed within the ducts. With the long endurance and high-speed cruise capacity of the XB-70, designers felt that it was particularly well suited for the RAM endurance and radar-suppression test flights. Tests were needed to measure the detectability of the XB-70 and other large high-performance aircraft by radars and infrared seekers, both with and without suppression aids. Radar suppression would have been tested by placing the RAM material in the air inlet ducts to diminish the reflected radar energy. Infrared suppression was to be tested by coating the XB-70 skin with material that could suppress infrared energy at tactically pivotal wave lengths.

Ground radar was to be used in trying to determine the radar cross-section (RCS) differences in several radar frequency ranges. The information gathered at different air intake duct ramp configurations would determine the effect of duct shape on RCS. From this, researchers could determine the effectiveness and the durability of the RAM coating. The effect of the RAM coating on skin temperature and structural integrity would also be measured by onboard instrumentation.

Of course, RCS was one of the tough selling points of the XB-70. She looked like a barn on the radar screen. After the U-2 was shot down in May 1960, RCS became an even bigger issue. So it is no surprise that designers planned to make the XB-70 look smaller.

WISH LIST TESTING

Astro-Observatory: The task description written for Valkyrie AV-3 cited plans for it to be used as a high-altitude observatory. That aircraft would have been equipped with astronomical gear and would fly to locations advantageous for observation and recording astronomical events such as solar eclipses. It was explained that the greater the flying observatory's velocity, the longer an eclipse could be viewed. At Mach 3.0, 8 minutes are available for viewing compared to 4.5 minutes at Mach 1.0. In addition to longer viewing times, the higher a flying observatory goes, the less atmospheric absorption there is, and cloud cover is no longer an issue. The XB-70 was the only high-performance vehicle that was stable enough and could carry the necessary payload to support such a project.

Despite the merits of the project, it too fell by the wayside. The United States pursued larger observatories on the ground. It wasn't until the launch of the Hubble Space Telescope decades later that the United States finally gained a high-altitude perch from which to view the stars.

A Recoverable Booster: One version of a production B-70 could have been used as a recoverable booster system to launch things into low earth orbit. Likely candidates included a proposed satellite-interceptor and the Aerospace Plane. The DynaSoar program, the first effort by the United States to use a manned boost-glider to fly in near orbital space and return, was also considered in this context in November 1959. The B-70 was to carry the 10,000-pound DynaSoar glider and a 40,000-pound liquid rocket booster to 70,000 feet and release them while traveling at Mach 3. With this lofty start, the booster could then push the glider into its final 300-mile orbit.

There were a few technical problems to overcome. A weight issue had to be wrestled with, since the B-70 would have been overweight in order to accomplish the launch. It was also the first time that the Air Force tried to merge missile, space, and aeronautical sciences into one package, so many issues of communication and compatibility had to be addressed.

Had the system ever been completed, it would have had the capability to carry its payload anywhere for launch and positioning—a useful feature when inclement weather threatens a launch schedule. With the current shuttle system, a launch must be delayed if the weather over the launch pad or in an emergency recovery area is not favorable, resulting in the loss of hours or days.

Satellite Killer: The B-70 Satellite Killer was to be the ultimate aircraft to both inspect and intercept enemy satellites in orbit. The B-70 would carry missiles or drones to the upper atmosphere for launch against orbiting targets. Missiles would be taken from existing stock in the Air Force inventory.

Static and Fatigue Tests of Components: The B-70 was a unique airframe, which presented an opportunity to explore static and fatigue problems and extremely complex loading of the aircraft. It was hoped that these tests would lead to design answers concerning the AMPSS and the SST. Static and fatigue testing would have scrutinized the forward fuselage, wing panels, horizontal stabilizer, and the landing gear.

Testing would also evaluate the closed-loop engine inlet shock wave controls to monitor unstart conditions. The aim was to limit the violent buffeting of the aircraft that resulted from the loss of shock wave positioning in the engine inlet. This test would allow evaluation of inlet control signals that could provide the information needed to record inlet air currents. Ambitious as it sounded, the information from this test would develop the SST and AMPSS inlet control and propulsion system and help limit the effects of jet wash or turbulence caused by one supersonic aircraft passing another.

Low-Altitude Penetration: When an Air Force general suggested to the head of North American Aviation, James H. "Dutch" Kindelberger, that the

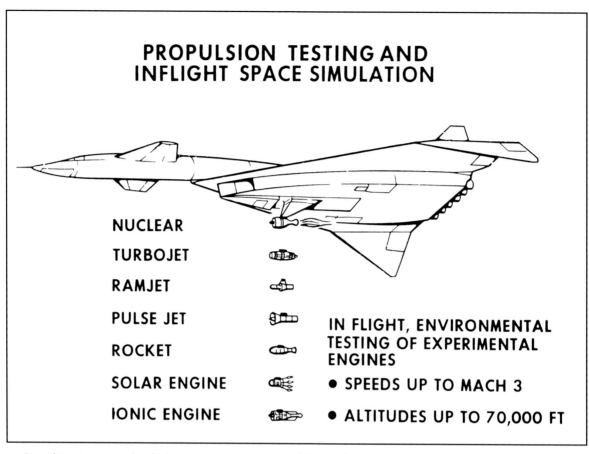

PROPULSION TESTING AND INFLIGHT SPACE SIMULATION

NUCLEAR

TURBOJET

RAMJET

PULSE JET

ROCKET

SOLAR ENGINE

IONIC ENGINE

IN FLIGHT, ENVIRONMENTAL TESTING OF EXPERIMENTAL ENGINES

• SPEEDS UP TO MACH 3

• ALTITUDES UP TO 70,000 FT

Propulsion testing and in-flight space simulation: part of the "wish list" for AV-3. *AFMC/HO*

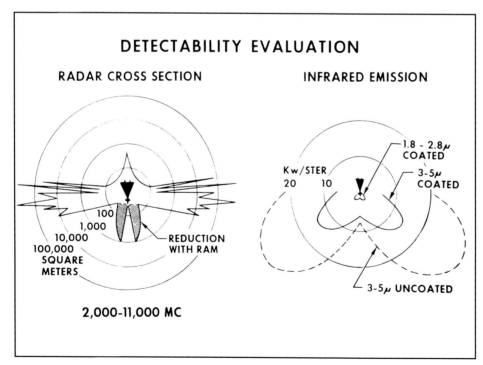

DETECTABILITY EVALUATION

RADAR CROSS SECTION

INFRARED EMISSION

100
1,000
10,000
100,000
SQUARE
METERS

REDUCTION WITH RAM

2,000-11,000 MC

1.8 - 2.8μ COATED

3-5μ COATED

Kw/STER
20   10

3-5μ UNCOATED

One of the ideas considered for AV-3 was the application of RAM (Radar Absorbent Material) coatings to reduce the Valkyrie's radar cross-section. *AFMC/HO*

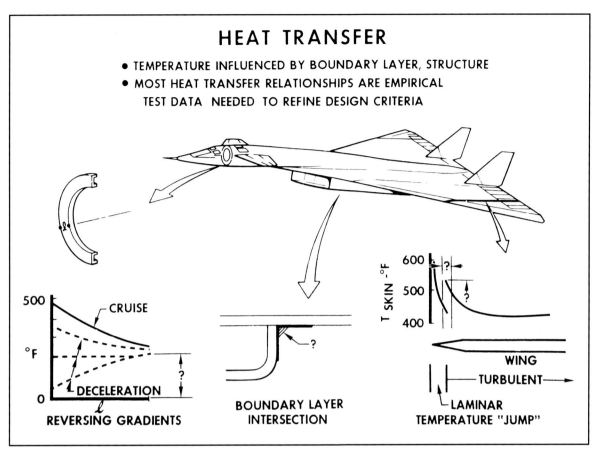

HEAT TRANSFER

- TEMPERATURE INFLUENCED BY BOUNDARY LAYER, STRUCTURE
- MOST HEAT TRANSFER RELATIONSHIPS ARE EMPIRICAL
  TEST DATA NEEDED TO REFINE DESIGN CRITERIA

REVERSING GRADIENTS

BOUNDARY LAYER INTERSECTION

TEMPERATURE "JUMP"

Heat buildup during flight at high Mach numbers was always a major concern. AV-3 would have been used to gather more test data to evaluate its effects. *AFMC/HO*

B-70's high-altitude mission was too dangerous due to the SAM threat, he decided to investigate low-altitude penetration. The purpose of the investigation was to see if the pilot and the aircraft could respond to the environment of near-supersonic speed at low altitude in enemy territory. Test pilots were to fly the B-70 at Mach .95 at sea level and evaluate the effect of speed and clearance attitudes, predict the ability to avoid terrain, and detect ground defense sites. The justification for it all was to recommend low-level capability for a B-70 type of design. Ultimately, similar high-speed missions were flown years later by the Rockwell B-1B Lancer.

Air Defense Evaluation: This program was to help estimate the defense of the United States and to provide information for the improvement of air defense systems. With new antennas and other countermeasure systems installed in the bomb bay, the military was to test and evaluate U.S. defense systems against threats, including manned enemy penetrators. The large payload capacity of the B-70 was to allow for many different types of countermeasure systems to be tested from subsonic to Mach 3 at high altitudes. It was hoped that one

aircraft would be able to simulate each of the different manned penetrators that were considered to be potential threats in the future.

Communications: Performance of communications equipment when working at high altitude and high speed was also considered for study. The tests would use the XB-70's AN/ARC-50 UHF set and the AN/ARN-65 TACAN (with the addition of a power amplifier) to show the increased communication range afforded by the high altitude. The tests would aid SST as well as military research. Testing would also encompass evaluation of supersonic static discharge—a critical factor in communications noise reduction. The tests were to be done in two phases: Part I to measure and record field strengths and discharge currents, and Part II to determine the static discharge device's field life.

Panel Response: Aircraft panel response to flutter and dynamic pressures from outside disturbances was an aeronautical issue at any speed. In the world of high-speed flight and the threat of unstarts, it was of grave concern. Instrumentation was to be provided to measure the effects that occurred from acoustical forces. Noise-measuring

COMPONENT DRAG INSTRUMENTATION

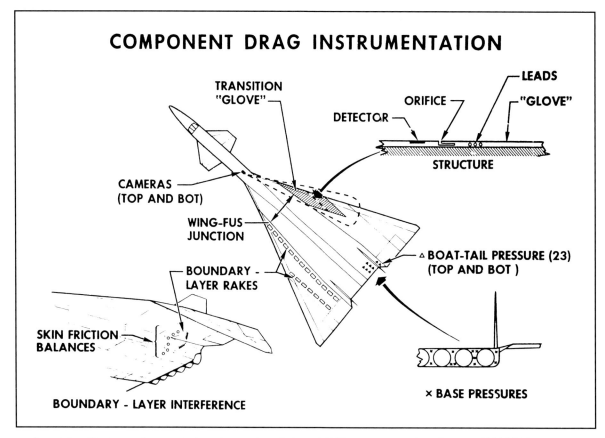

A variety of instruments were to have been placed aboard AV-3 to measure drag factors. *AFMC/HO*

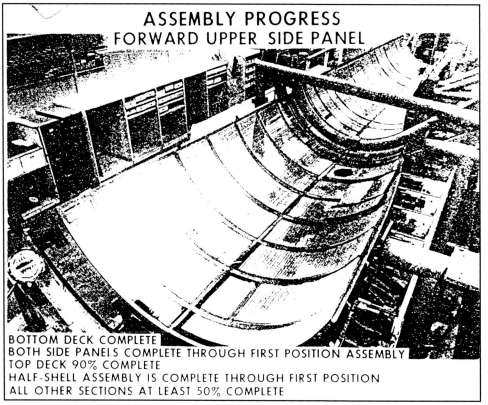

ASSEMBLY PROGRESS
FORWARD UPPER SIDE PANEL

BOTTOM DECK COMPLETE
BOTH SIDE PANELS COMPLETE THROUGH FIRST POSITION ASSEMBLY
TOP DECK 90% COMPLETE
HALF-SHELL ASSEMBLY IS COMPLETE THROUGH FIRST POSITION
ALL OTHER SECTIONS AT LEAST 50% COMPLETE

Assembly of the third Valkyrie in progress. *AFMC/HO*

instruments, including microphones, transducers, and even thermocouples, were to be mounted in high-noise-level areas such as the aft fuselage and the engine inlets. This test would not require any excess flight time and was to be done during normal flight procedures.

Crew Protection and Environment:
A crew protection and environment study was to evaluate the crew under various circumstances and tolerance levels to determine the type of protection required. Environment was the heading under which temperature, pressure, air composition, and workload were measured. Radiation levels in the upper atmosphere were also a concern due to the sharp increase in exposure noted at higher levels.

Advanced Flight Controls:
High-speed and altitude operation, fuselage flexibility, air vehicle size, landing attitude and speed, and extended temperature and pressure environments were all issues needing exploration. Adaptive control systems were beneficial to the evaluation of the AMPSS and SST, the automatic landing systems, and the emergency descent capsule used for in-flight emergencies.

Weapons and Components Testing Research:
Weapons and components testing research was to aid in the design of new ordnance, missiles, and components for use in supersonic aircraft. Environmental data would be gained for the effects of aerodynamic heating, vibration, acoustics, and G load. Instrumentation would provide for weapon ejection shock, safe separation, and trajectory. The tests would also provide information pertaining to in-flight platform alignment of inertial guided missiles, missile delivery accuracy, and ballistic determination of supersonic gravity-dropped ordnance. Since the XB-70 was the only aircraft capable of performing in this high-speed, high-altitude theater, its navigation system was unique in that it could provide weapons release data for advanced weapons systems.

Navigation and Guidance System:
The B-70 was to be used to study the effects of high altitude and high speed on navigation performance, including Stellar-Doppler inertial, Doppler inertial, pure Doppler, and pure inertial radars. The ability of a Doppler radar to lock on to a usable ground return signal at high speed and high altitudes needed to be determined. The designers also planned to evaluate the stellar monitor which, if it were to be used in any high-speed, high-altitude regime, needed to function properly. The XB-70 could create a shock wave severe enough to effect refraction of light going to the stellar monitor. The XB-70 was the only aircraft that could fly this regime that was already equipped with Stellar-Doppler inertial navigation system.

Supersonic Refueling:
Supersonic refueling was to precipitate the need for refueling high-speed aircraft. The study would determine the feasibility and develop the technique for fuel transfer at supersonic speed. The test vehicle modifications were to be based on the results of wind tunnel, flight simulator, and flight tests and would consist of a "dry hookup" between the XB-70 and another supersonic aircraft (perhaps another B-70), simulating a tanker.

High-Speed Launch Vehicle:
The B-70 was considered as a high-altitude launch vehicle to obtain data on spacecraft configuration. Full-scale lifting body spacecraft (both manned and unmanned) would be attached to the B-70, carried aloft, and dropped at various airspeeds and altitudes. Once launched scientists would study the spacecraft's stability and control characteristics, effects of drag, maximum drop speeds attainable, and landing speed data. It would provide actual data on spacecraft pilot training, lifting body flying characteristics, and control data from supersonic flight speed to landing.

RSB-70

Not much has been written about a proposal for a reconnaissance-strike bomber, put forward in the mid-1960s, that attempted to save the B-70 program from extinction. The proposal came to light after being declassified in August 1997. It was a last-ditch effort to save some of the development work already done in the B-70 program.

The cover letter accompanying the proposal notes that its purpose was to clarify for Air Force commanders the Air Force's stand on the operational status of the B-70 program. It was meant to complement the ballistic missiles that were coming on board in droves, and it also addressed the reconnaissance issue. It should be noted that during the same time, the Lockheed Skunk Works' A-12 program was already in progress, with a first flight coming soon, and the U-2 was already in service.

The Air Force hoped to convince the Department of Defense, and its leader, Robert McNamara, that the XB-70 was a versatile aircraft. Some of the conceptual modifications in the aircraft's subsystems had already been made, or were just about ready to be made, and the implication was that the B-70 could be fielded quickly with those changes. The listing of changes for the "new version B-70," the Reconnaissance Strike B-70, were:

1. The B-70's deployment strategy would allow wider and more variable dispersal to enhance initial attack survival and subsequent transattack operations.
2. The role of the RSB-70 would be augmented to provide reconnaissance and damage assessment information, on both enemy and U.S. forces, to U.S. command authority.

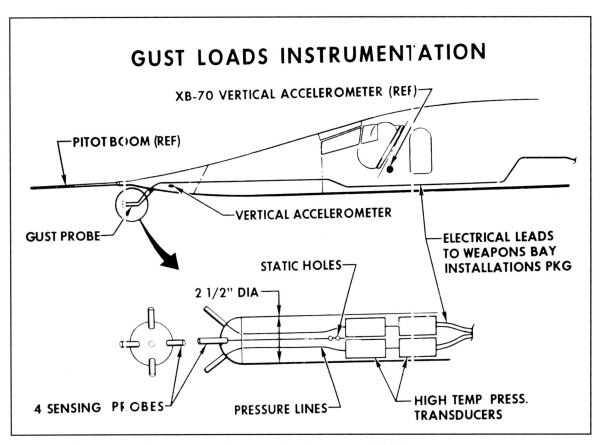

GUST LOADS INSTRUMENTATION

XB-70 VERTICAL ACCELEROMETER (REF)

PITOT BOOM (REF)

VERTICAL ACCELEROMETER

ELECTRICAL LEADS
TO WEAPONS BAY
INSTALLATIONS PKG

GUST PROBE

STATIC HOLES

2 1/2" DIA

4 SENSING PROBES

PRESSURE LINES

HIGH TEMP. PRESS.
TRANSDUCERS

Gust loads instrumentation chart shows placement of accelerometers. *AFMC/HO*

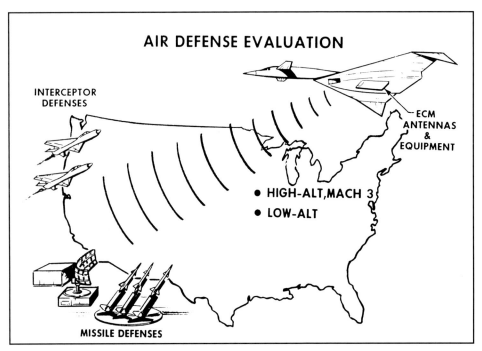

AIR DEFENSE EVALUATION

INTERCEPTOR
DEFENSES

ECM
ANTENNAS
&
EQUIPMENT

● HIGH-ALT, MACH 3
● LOW-ALT

MISSILE DEFENSES

Air defense evalua-
tion chart shows
interceptor defense,
ECM antennas and
equipment, and
high-altitude Mach
3 vs. low-altitude
missile defenses.
AFMC/HO

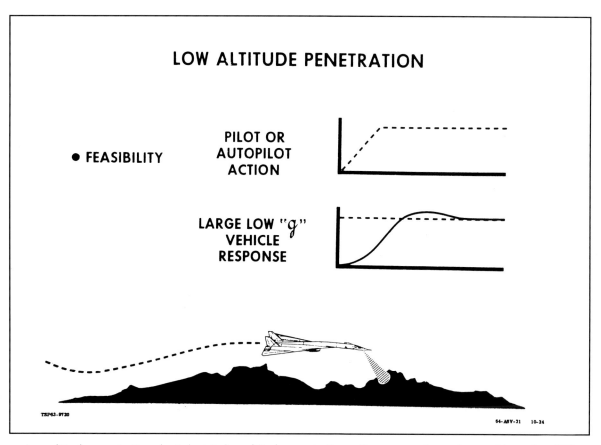

LOW ALTITUDE PENETRATION

● FEASIBILITY

PILOT OR AUTOPILOT ACTION

LARGE LOW "g" VEHICLE RESPONSE

TSP63-9720   64-A6V-31   10-24

Low-altitude penetration chart depicts low-altitude penetration, pilot or autopilot action, and large low-"G" vehicle feasibility. *AFMC/HO*

3. Changes in mission tactics would exploit the new roles, support a change in armament, and improve penetration capability of the aircraft.
4. Changes in aircraft subsystems would contribute to improved reconnaissance sensors and more reliable command communications for reconnaissance reporting and force control.
5. Highly accurate air-to-ground strike missiles would be developed as substitutes for free-fall bombs.

RSB-70 operations would be staged differently from those of the original B-70 bomber configuration. The Air Force tried to emphasize that a variety of responses would be available under different degrees of international tensions and military alerts, with the purpose being to disperse the aircraft and prepare them for attack. It also provided better recall value, something that the Mutually Assured Destruction (MAD) philosophy did not and could never provide.

The new operational concept, known as the "Strike Force Team," used KC-135s to escort RSB-70s from ground alert to airborne loiter over prearranged points and positioning at forward bases. (Much the same system was used in SR-71 deployments.) The KC-135 would provide maintenance personnel, aircraft spares, and equipment for

a self-contained turnaround capability. Tanker crews would live aboard the KC-135, and fuel could be transferred to the aircraft on the ground or in the air. Extra weapons would also be carried aboard the support aircraft. Of course, the refueling system on the RSB-70 had not yet been developed, but it would have been fitted to the third B-70 (AV-3), in a configuration that would have been closer to the full production model than that of the other two B-70s.

Aircraft would have been able to deploy to any site that could support an RSB-70 takeoff and landing, where it would either remain on site, or launch to an airborne loiter point. A runway of at least 11,000 feet was required, and at the time there were at least 110 airfields in the United States that had adequate runway length for a full gross weight takeoff. Additional airfields could support reduced-weight takeoffs, with postlaunch aerial refueling to support the RSB-70 in much the same way as the SR-71. The Air Force came up with a total of 300 airfields that could be used to support the program.

Should there have been an alert, at least 75 percent of the Strike Force Team would deploy with no more than two or three teams per landing site. Due to the large number of sites available, problems encountered by partially destroyed bases would default to prepositioned fuel and support equipment at various sites to maintain high-level support. All the RSB-70s would be equipped with ultra high frequency (UHF), high-frequency single sideband (HF SSB), and low-frequency (LF) receivers to provide for receipt of command messages and for redirection of aircraft under the management of commanding officers.

With the threat of a full-scale attack, the complete complement of Strike Force Teams would go to an airborne loiter situation. This would put the RSB-70s teams safely in the air, allowing designated aircraft to be sent out on missions or redirected to remote landing sites, or remain in airborne loiter to do bomb damage assessment and gather details on the effects of enemy strikes on U.S. cities.

Offensive Subsystems and Weapons - The XB-70 was built with some of the systems already in place, so it would not take much to implement the full RS capability in an operational fleet. The Automatic Flight Control System (AFCS) would allow crew members to concentrate more on the reconnaissance task at hand instead of flying the aircraft. There was a "focused radar" that had been installed and tested in the XB-70 already that improved resolution from 150-200 feet to 10-30 feet.

One of the biggest changes was the inclusion of guided strike missiles instead of free-fall bombs. Due to the missile guidance, the B-70's weapons delivery accuracy would improve from the original 3,000-foot CEP (circular error of probability) to a 600-foot CEP. This offered a more selective destruction of targets, and increased the weapons payload effectiveness for a single mission.

Two types of missiles were chosen for the RSB-70. The first was a glide weapon that used the XB-70's Mach 3 capability and 70,000-foot ceiling from which to launch. The glide missile would have a guidance system that could put a 400-kiloton warhead within five feet of the target. The second system would be rocket-boosted for higher speeds and longer range. It would carry a 200-kiloton warhead for softer targets and defense installations. Using strike missiles in this fashion would save the RSB-70 from having to fly over enemy territory and limit exposure to enemy defenses. Whichever system was chosen, it would have required two crew members to fill the new rolls of Reconnaissance Navigation Officer and Weapons Officer.

A few other subsystems were to be modified and upgraded as well. Infrared (IR) and low-light-level TV sensors would be added, in addition to a radar direction finder (RDF) for detecting the location of enemy defense radars.

Survival over Enemy Territory - Since the RSB-70 was to exist in a world filled with ICBMs that did not risk the lives of crew or need to return to base, its ability to survive over enemy territory was frequently called into question. The RSB-70's missile capability would keep it from flying directly over enemy targets. With its large

weapons load and long-range missiles, it could strike a variety of targets from a standoff position.

Proponents argued that the RSB-70 offered a recall capability. There would be constant communication for command and control of airborne aircraft, offering a wide range of options for managing various levels of tension and warning situations. The RSB-70 also offered on-site bomb damage assessment. This information would relay through the KC-135, which would act as refueler and a forward controller to get information to other airborne RSB-70s and airborne command posts.

Cost-Effectiveness - To further argue its case, the Air Force compared the RSB-70's cost-effectiveness to the ICBM missile systems on the drawing boards. The Minuteman missile was a cost-effective, quick-reaction weapon that lived in underground, hardened silos, and was basically secure against anything except a massive attack and a direct hit. The submarine-launched Polaris missile was an excellent deterrent system for keeping escalation in check because of its near invulnerability, but it was much more expensive on a cost-per-kill basis.

When determining the costs, the Air Force was very specific in outlining the role of the RSB-70. The program was intended to "furnish elements of discrimination and precision, force management visibility through selective reconnaissance, and a wide choice of force application processes." The use of a large number of strike missiles and improved survival techniques would make the RSB-70 competitive with any ballistic missile system on a cost-per-kill basis, and expand the force mix of manned bombers and ballistic missiles that the Air Force wanted.

OPERATING COSTS

In light of today's development budgets, it really would not have cost that much to keep the XB-70 program operational. It would have cost the U.S. taxpayers $5.5 million to keep at least one Valkyrie working at approximately 100 hours of test flight. To keep two of them working would have cost approximately $8.2 million, with operation of both for 100 hours of test flight. The cost to include spare engines would add another $2.5 million, with $1 million a year in advance to support General Electric engines.

The whole program was estimated to have cost $1.5 billion for prototype development costs. It was actually more expensive to cancel the third air vehicle because it drove up the manufacturing costs, not to mention the extra costs to maintain the flight test program with two aircraft. Cancellation of the third aircraft was not really a wise thing to do if you looked at the proposed figures.

The contractors and the Air Force were willing to do their share to keep the program going; however, Kennedy and McNamara were not willing to allow it, no matter what Congress thought. John Kennedy, in a pre-election

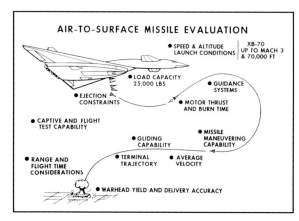

AIR-TO-SURFACE MISSILE EVALUATION

- SPEED & ALTITUDE LAUNCH CONDITIONS | XB-70 UP TO MACH 3 & 70,000 FT
- LOAD CAPACITY 25,000 LBS
- EJECTION CONSTRAINTS
- GUIDANCE SYSTEMS
- MOTOR THRUST AND BURN TIME
- CAPTIVE AND FLIGHT TEST CAPABILITY
- GLIDING CAPABILITY
- MISSILE MANEUVERING CAPABILITY
- RANGE AND FLIGHT TIME CONSIDERATIONS
- TERMINAL TRAJECTORY
- AVERAGE VELOCITY
- WARHEAD YIELD AND DELIVERY ACCURACY

Air-to-surface missile evaluation chart. Parameters depicted are: speed and altitude launch conditions, load capacity of 25,000 pounds ejection constraints, motor thrust and burn time, guidance systems, captive and flight test capability, range and flight time considerations, gliding capability, missile maneuvering capability, terminal trajectory, average velocity, warhead yield, and delivery accuracy. *AFMC/HO*

SUPERSONIC REFUELING
-FEASIBILITY-

- RENDEZVOUS
- HOOK-UP
- CONTROL

- DETERMINE CRITERIA TECHNIQUES

Supersonic refueling feasibility chart suggests rendezvous, hookup, and control issues and indicates the need to determine criteria and techniques for successful in-flight refueling. *AFMC/HO*

speech to aerospace workers, promised to keep the XB-70 dream alive. He didn't keep the promise. In spite of that, were are still reaping rewards from the XB-70 today.

THE SEARCH FOR THE THIRD VALKYRIE

In early 1997, evidence suggested that pieces of the third aircraft might have been found at Plant 42 in Palmdale, California. A security guard at Plant 42 (who is also an XB-70 buff) went to look at the material, which was discovered at Site 8 in the plant. While he was holding a rather large and square fuel gauge (which was typical of fuel gauges of 1960's vintage aircraft), he asked an individual from the site if the gauge could have come from among the bits and pieces of the third Valkyrie.

He was assured that it had, but it later turned out to be a gauge from a B-2 mockup. All was not lost however, as he was told that there were probably other pieces in the area since the

remains of AV-3 had long ago been moved there from Site 3. Roughly 20,000 to 30,000 pounds of material belonging to the third Valkyrie had reportedly been scrapped out about four or five years earlier. After further investigation, the guard apparently found a cockpit section from the aircraft. Perhaps it might have been part of the wooden mockup of the XB-70, which had disappeared with the rest of the program material about the same time the XB-70 program was shut down. However, when asked if it was possible that the mockup had survived, the chief designer for the XB-70 said the mockup was also lost to posterity.

The disposition of the Valkyrie's engines was also researched, and it was discovered that, of the 31 YJ-93-3 engines built for the program, only 17 could be accounted for. Apparently, there are no records available showing the serial numbers, nor are there records showing any actions that may have been taken to scrap the engines. They simply don't appear in any inventory list. At last report, General Electric Aircraft Engines was still researching this matter.

CHAPTER 9

View of Tu-144 landing with nose in lowered position. *NASA*

The SST and The XB-70

Just what does SST mean? It stands for supersonic transport, which is an all-encompassing term for a passenger-carrying aircraft that can fly at a sustained cruise speed of Mach 1 or better, usually Mach 2, with the purpose of shortening flight times between continents. The SST would use regular air traffic lanes, except when higher altitude was required for Mach flight, and would need to use the larger international airports to support her runway and service needs. The SST was to be a viable commercial venture for the airlines, and for the country supporting her development.

Back in the heyday of exploration into supersonic commercial flight, the French, British, and Russians all were attempting to come up with the consummate high-speed aircraft. Due to the similarities in their initial designs and projected high costs, the French and British joined forces and decided to build their SST together, ultimately producing the Concorde. The Russians went their own route and developed the Tu-144. On June 4, 1963, Pan American Airways decided to purchase six SSTs from the Anglo-French concern. Pan Am's original SST order, coupled with the knowledge that the Russians were also building the Tu-144, spurred the United States to get into the game. Pan Am later canceled their order in favor of the new Boeing 747, but the stage was already set. President Kennedy announced: "If we can build the best operational airplane of this type and I believe that we can, then the congress of this country should be prepared to invest funds and the efforts necessary to maintain the national lead in long-range aircraft, a lead which we have held since the second world war, a lead which we should make every responsible effort to maintain." Thus the United States entered the fray for developing commercial high-speed flight.

Supersonic flight had to be "user-friendly" and the XB-70 program was attempting to supply some solutions. She was ready-made for the position. In 1963, the first Valkyrie was well on the way to completion, with her two sisters not far behind. At the time, the XB-70 program was having financial problems because of arguments between Congress and the DOD. NASA was happy to jump on board and fund the testing with the idea that it might be a good way to bolster the SST program. There were many problems to be solved before an American SST could be built.

In 1965, the United States had not yet come up with accurate wind tunnel models, so it had difficulty estimating the base drag of a multiengine aircraft. The XB-70 was to run these tests live, during regular flight. Tests called for cameras to be placed on the fuselage so in-flight photographs could be taken to resolve boundary layer transition pattern issues. Later on, a wing glove would be installed, permitting the study of the effects of roughness on airflow, especially during the subsonic-transonic-super-

AERO-THERMO-ELASTICITY INSTRUMENTATION

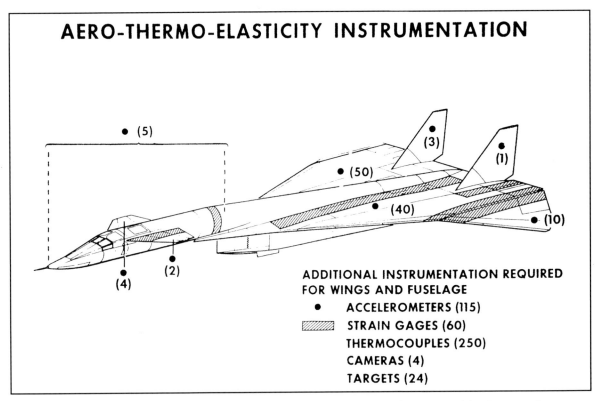

ADDITIONAL INSTRUMENTATION REQUIRED FOR WINGS AND FUSELAGE

- ● ACCELEROMETERS (115)
- ▨ STRAIN GAGES (60)
- THERMOCOUPLES (250)
- CAMERAS (4)
- TARGETS (24)

Aero-thermo-elasticity instrumentation. Additional instrumentation required for wings and fuselage: accelerometer positions (115), strain gauges (60), thermocouples (250), cameras (4), and targets (24). *AFMC/HO*

SST ENGINE FLIGHT TESTING

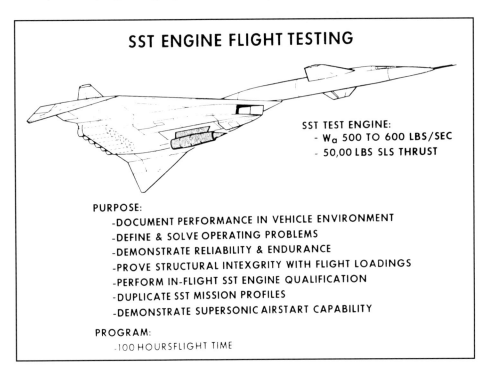

SST TEST ENGINE:
- W_a 500 TO 600 LBS/SEC
- 50,00 LBS SLS THRUST

PURPOSE:
- DOCUMENT PERFORMANCE IN VEHICLE ENVIRONMENT
- DEFINE & SOLVE OPERATING PROBLEMS
- DEMONSTRATE RELIABILITY & ENDURANCE
- PROVE STRUCTURAL INTEXGRITY WITH FLIGHT LOADINGS
- PERFORM IN-FLIGHT SST ENGINE QUALIFICATION
- DUPLICATE SST MISSION PROFILES
- DEMONSTRATE SUPERSONIC AIRSTART CAPABILITY

PROGRAM:
- 100 HOURS FLIGHT TIME

The SST engine flight test program had many objectives including performance documentation, problem definition, reliability demonstration, and the exploration of potential SST mission profiles. *AFMC/HO*

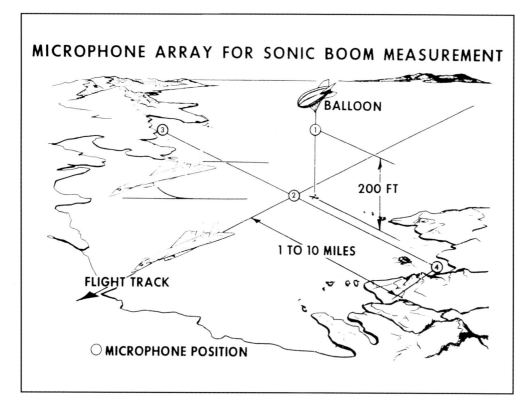

MICROPHONE ARRAY FOR SONIC BOOM MEASUREMENT

BALLOON

200 FT

1 TO 10 MILES

FLIGHT TRACK

○ MICROPHONE POSITION

The chart for placement of the sonic boom measurement microphone array shows vectors, flight track, and microphone position. *AFMC/HO*

NASA-FAA RESEARCH PROGRAM

AERODYNAMICS

SKIN FRICTION-BASE DRAG
BOUNDARY LAYER TRANSITION
INTERNAL AERODYNAMICS
FLIGHT CONTROL-HANDLING QUALITIES

STRUCTURES

AERO-THERMO-ELASTICITY
LANDING LOADS
PANEL RESPONSE-BOUNDARY LAYER NOISE
GUST LOADS

OPERATIONS

SIMULATED AIRLINE OPERATIONS
SYSTEMS EVALUATION
SONIC BOOM AND RUNWAY NOISE
SST ENGINE QUALIFICATION TESTS

The NASA/FAA Research Program covered many areas of investigation. *AFMC/HO*

XB-70 AV-1 shows vortex contrails during NASA flights at Mach speeds. *NASA*

sonic transition. The glove would allow the leading edge to be varied to investigate a combination of effects. Thermocouples, or temperature resistance gauges, installed in the glove would provide additional data.

The SST program was trying to define a realistic design for the SST based on what was learned from the XB-70. Designers discovered, later in the program testing of the XB-70, that they had missed the aerodynamic design range by possibly as much as 25 percent. This discrepancy was due to a problem with wind tunnel data interpretation. The designers had overestimated the lift-to-drag ratio, underestimated the transonic drag, then underestimated the inlet performance. It was simply a matter of wind tunnel evaluations being far from perfect.

Early in the XB-70 flight test program, NASA and the Air Force found out that the XB-70 could have some undesirable flying characteristics. Pilots found that the XB-70 was a "rudder airplane"—it demonstrated adverse yaw because of the aileron input—in all flight conditions. There was also negative dihedral effect at high speed. At high speeds, the negative dihedral caused a crosswise motion, creating large sideslip angles that were

undetectable to the pilots. Part of the XB-70's flight control system contained a stability augmentation system. When the XB-70 was flown with stability augmentation off, the pilots were able to control banking tendencies normally via rudder pedals. Armed with this knowledge, the SST would likely have been capable of easy flight with all augmentation off throughout its flight envelope.

Apparently, handling the XB-70 could be a tough business in unfavorable air conditions, but there wasn't anything like flying the XB-70 when the conditions were good. According to Al White in his first postflight interview, "she was made to fly." Due to the groundwork laid by the XB-70, many of the wind tunnel data testing procedures were revised and better testing methods were developed.

Weather was another consideration that had not been explored. Commercial flight is weather dependent and the SST would be, too. The SST could fly above weather, but she still had to go through it during departures and arrivals. The time spent in supersonic flight would be only 20 or 30 minutes at best. The atmospheric conditions prevailing at high altitudes were sure to affect Mach 3 SST operations. In tests with the XB-70, NASA and the Air Force found that their flight temperature predictions were

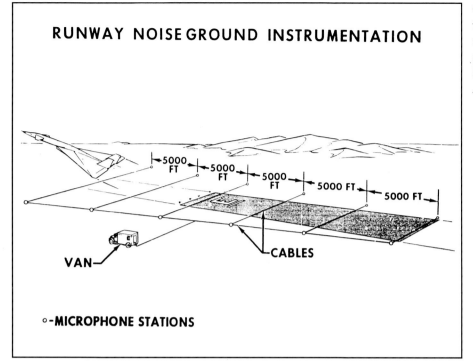

RUNWAY NOISE GROUND INSTRUMENTATION

5000 FT
5000 FT
5000 FT
5000 FT
5000 FT
VAN
CABLES
°-MICROPHONE STATIONS

Ground instrumentation to evaluate runway noise featured microphone stations at 5,000-foot intervals. *AFMC/HO*

SUMMARY - NATIONAL RESEARCH PROGRAM
CALENDAR YEARS

1965	1966	1967	1968	1969
AIRCRAFT CHECKOUT →	← RESEARCH FLIGHTS →		← RESEARCH FLIGHTS →	
	144 HOURS	MODIFICATION	100 HOURS	

CURRENT PGM AIR FORCE
- ENVELOPE EXPANSION
- GENERAL H.Q. |60 HOURS
- STRUCTURES
- INLET ENGINE, ETC.

NASA
- SKIN FRICTION
- BASE DRAG
- BOUNDARY LAYER NOISE |84 HOURS SIMULATED AIRLINE OPERATION
- PANEL RESPONSE
- GUST LOADS
- THERMAL ENVIRONMENT
- GENERAL H.Q.
- SONIC BOOM
- RUNWAY NOISE

LANDING LOADS A/V NO. 1

NASA -FAA RESEARCH
SKIN FRICTION
GUST LOADS
GENERAL H.Q.
SONIC BOOM
INTERNAL AERO-DYAMICS

INSTALL
- LAMINAR FLOW GLOVE
- CAMERAS
- AERO - THERMO ELASTIC INST.
- SST ENGINE *
- PERTINENT SST SYSTEMS *

- ADDITIONAL SIMULATED AIRLINE - 40 HOURS OPERATION
- BOUNDARY LAYER TRANSITION - 10 HOURS
- AERO - THERMO - ELASTIC PROGRAM - 50 HOURS
- FLIGHT QUALIFICATION OF SST ENGINE *   - (100 HOURS)
- SST SYSTEMS DEVELOPMENT *

* IF FEASIBLE

---

close to those actually experienced. However, XB-70 fuel consumption was higher than predicted and was a factor that would have to be carefully addressed in the SST. Tests showed that on a warm day, flight at a lower than optimum Mach number would adversely affect the fuel reserves. That meant that range would have to be refigured and greater allowances would need to be made for temperature

variations, even for altitudes of 60,000 feet or more. The effects of air turbulence had not been predicted with sufficient accuracy either, and that would be a pivotal factor affecting the supersonic performance.

Supersonic performance is also greatly influenced by the shape of an aircraft's nose and windscreen. The problem is that a highly aerodynamic nose is difficult to see out of.

Airborne view of British Airways Concorde SST. *British Airways*

One of the outstanding features of the XB-70 was her variable-position nose ramp, which could be lowered for improved pilot visibility at lower speeds, or raised to improve aerodynamics. These characteristics are advantageous for an SST as well, and similar mechanisms were built into the Tu-144 and Concorde. The XB-70's nose ramp could be operated at indicated airspeeds of up to 560 knots. She proved that she could fly with the ramp down at Mach 2.5 with little adverse effect and good visibility. The increased windshield drag with the ramp down only slightly reduced the optimum climb-speed performance (560 KIAS instead of a normal 575 KIAS). Since the nose ramp could be actuated rapidly, pilots could use it to gain a better view of the horizon in front of them. Some engineers speculated that the loss of speed was not worth better visibility because one did not need a good view when traveling at Mach 2.5 or beyond. The XB-70 pilots disagreed. The nose ramp gave them a chance to "see" their way around the sky instead of just "feel" it.

The XB-70 carried conventional round flight instrument dials as well as vertical-tape flight instruments, as in other aircraft such as the F-102 Delta Dagger. Either instrument type would serve the purpose, but most pilots were more comfortable with the round dials. There were several unique things about the XB-70 cockpit. There was a digital readout of air speed and altitude. There was also an EGT (exhaust gas temperature) gauge with a warning light to easily warn pilots of an over-temperature situation. Early in the XB-70's career there were no warning lights on the EGTs, and pilots sometimes overlooked a high-temperature reading. When this happened, engines had to be removed to check for overheats. In the view of the men who flew her, the installation of the new EGT saved several engines from potential damage, and they justified themselves many times over. EGT warnings would substantially reduce maintenance costs for an SST operator.

The XB-70 was difficult to maintain at a constant altitude at high speed. There was no autopilot on board, so that made it even more difficult to handle. At Mach 3.0 at 70,000 feet, an attitude change of just one degree changed the rate of climb as much as 3,000 feet per minute! A sonic boom test showed that it was difficult to hold altitude because of vertical and horizontal control interactions. It also showed that an attitude director with a pitch scale of double sensitivity gave better resolution and afforded easier altitude control. Only a few flights were flown with the

Rollout of the refurbished Russian Tu-144. *Boeing*

more sensitive attitude instrument, but it proved that it afforded better high-speed flying characteristics. These characteristics would provide more economical SST flight operations by saving fuel.

Other XB-70 tests ascertained that excessive speed was a definite problem that had to be addressed for SST operation. The XB-70 was normally accelerated to, and then climbed at 560 KIAS with the nose ramp down, or at 575 KIAS with nose ramp up. The XB-70 pilots had to keep her within the placarded limits for maximum speed due to design considerations. The exact climb schedule for the XB-70 was difficult to maintain even under the best circumstances. There were no overspeed warning devices installed on the XB-70, but tests showed that they would be necessary on the SST.

The XB-70 was built with airflow bypass doors and movable inlet panels to control the air going into the engines. This provided a means of bringing the normal supersonic shock wave inside each inlet at speeds above Mach 2.0 to maintain efficiency. When the normal shock wave is precisely positioned inside the inlet, the inlet is considered to be "started"; when that wave moves outside the inlet, it is considered to be "unstarted." An inlet unstart

is a sudden and very unpleasant event that causes airframe buffeting, engine stalls, inlet buzz, and other distracting motions and noises. SST passengers would likely object to being tossed around and frightened out of their wits during the 5 to 10 seconds that it took to restart an inlet, so XB-70 testing would be useful in modifying the unpleasant effects of unstarts through better inlet control and more reliable and automatic "restarting" systems.

The SST would operate in an environment that was decidedly unfriendly to noise, like anywhere over the continental United States, for example. The FAA would have to make provisions for SST noise abatement during take-off and landing. Since engine noise can be translated into engine power output, the XB-70's engine's decibel levels were kept classified to hide their output levels from the Soviets. Even so, anyone near an Air Force base where an XB-70 was operating knew the YJ-93s were anything but quiet. The SST would need similar power to the XB-70, but not all the noise.

The XB-70's landing sequence showed the importance of precision in deceleration and descent planning to SST operations. Descent from Mach 2.7 cruise flight had to begin 200 nautical miles from the destination for

Russian generals posing beside the Tu-144 with the logos of the various corporations involved in its resurrection. *Boeing*

the aircraft to be subsonic at the correct distance and altitude to permit its incorporation into subsonic jet traffic. At a speed of 27 nautical miles per minute, it was essential that the pilot had the appropriate clearances before arriving at the deceleration point. Sonic boom avoidance was added to the equation as a speed of Mach 1.0 or below had to be achieved before the aircraft descended below 35,000 feet.

The XB-70 had its share of landing gear problems. It was shown in test flights that landing gear for the SST would have to be of a simple design. The XB-70's landing gear locked up on the first flight, and in another instance the emergency landing gear system had to be activated to get the gear "down and locked."

If nose gear should fail in the XB-70, the only recourse would have been to bail out. There was not going to be a bailout feature in the SST. Through all the XB-70's trials and tribulations with landing gear problems, it was shown that the SST needed to have an emergency extension system that had a pneumatic or hydraulic back-up. It had to be a system that the crew and a couple of hundred passengers could rely on.

Hydraulic system leaks abounded in the early XB-70 program. At first, there were hydraulic pressure gauges in the cockpit, but no hydraulic quantity gauges. The XB-70 pilots were not too pleased with this configuration and demanded that they be installed before the first flight. Because of their insistence, hydraulic leaks could be detected in the cockpit and coped with via fluid transfer between hydraulic systems and replenishment from a 30-gallon tank reservoir with an electric pump. This system of gauges and reservoir helped reduce the need for emergency landings and contamination of the hydraulic system from cavitation. It was thought that the SST should have some sort of hydraulic quantity gauges and some type of replenishment system.

The XB-70 under ideal circumstances was not a difficult plane to land. Because of her stability and good engine response (with the help of the electric throttle system), airspeed could be maintained within two knots of the required aim speed. Experience gained from the XB-70's high approach speed of 200 knots revealed that it would be difficult to land an SST at the same rate. XB-70 testing showed that the lower the approach and landing speed of the SST, the easier the landing workload would be for the pilots.

There were to be many other tests on the XB-70 for skin friction, base drag, boundary layer transitions, inlet aerodynamics, flight control handling including stability tests, and control derivatives. In the structural area, all efforts were made to try to understand the thermoelastic phenomenon along with efforts to understand landing load, panel response, and the gust load issues. Operations research included tests that simulated airline operations, sonic booms, and runway noise evaluation. The airspeed calibration tests and sonic boom runs in particular were performed minutes prior to the accident that took AV-2 on June 8, 1966.

There was some hope that the XB-70 would eventually serve as a test bed for SST engines. The plan for the SST engine testing was fairly expansive, but much could be learned about in-flight SST engine qualifications even within a 100-hour flight test program. Some of the other items needing in-flight research were structural integrity, flight loading, mission profiles, overall reliability, and endurance.

The SST program was trying to define a realistic design for the SST, based on what was learned from the XB-70. The XB-70, even in the pared-down program with reduced funding, proved to be a success. Problems unique to the Mach 3 flight of a large airliner were easily demonstrated by XB-70 flight tests. Once the problems were known, solutions would soon follow. The XB-70 made a large contribution to the United State's SST research.

CHAPTER 10

A full-length view of the XB-70 on Ohio Route 444 as she is towed to the USAF Museum past historic Huffman Dam. The move was carefully planned and traffic was stopped for quite some time. Note that the massive rudders have been removed, leaving only the stubs of the vertical stabilizers. *USAF Museum*

The Last Flight

A MEMOIR BY JOE VENTOLO, JR.

The weather was crisp and clear the afternoon of February 4, 1969. With our bosses' blessing, John, Bill, and I were taking a break from the seemingly endless task of looking at official Air Force motion picture footage on clattering Movieola film editing machines. (The job description called it "motion picture film evaluation.") Now, we hoped, we'd see something in person that we'd seen before only on film. The North American XB-70 Valkyrie was making its last flight today to join the collection of the U.S. Air Force Museum at Wright-Patterson Air Force Base. We wanted to see the final landing.

So the three of us hopped into John's car and drove the four miles to the main runway area at Patterson Field. There we found a suitable vantage point from which to witness the XB-70's last touchdown; it was one of Wright-Patt's small "pocket" parks, this one situated at the edge of the military golf course and about a quarter mile or so from the main runway. We could see both ends of the 12,600-foot-long slab of concrete, so visibility would not be a problem. But the way the wind was blowing meant that we were a good two miles from the approach end. None of us had thought to bring a camera, though. Or binoculars. This would be strictly an eyeball experience.

For a time it appeared our wait would be a long one. We had chosen not to go to the official viewing area hoping to avoid the crowds, and in so choosing we had no access to any updated word on the actual time of the Valkyrie's arrival. It didn't matter. The temperature was reasonable, we were suitably bundled up, and at least we were out of our windowless offices. And, for a short time, we were away from the infernal clatter of those damned Movieolas.

Most of the time, those seasick-green tools of our trade were nothing more than subtle instruments of torture, but over the years they had given us our first close-up, uncut, on-film views of the astonishingly beautiful flying machine we were waiting to see now with our own eyes—not as a tiny, flickering image. Sure, there had been plenty of press photos, and lots of publicity—some of it bad—printed about the XB-70, but none of the photos published in magazines or shown on TV were quite as detailed as what we motion picture archivists saw while cranking through thousands of feet of film.

We figured that our first clue of the Valkyrie's imminent arrival would be signs of increased activity on the field close to the runway. We were right! Before long, Air Force vehicles of assorted sizes and shapes began racing here and there, their flashing lights giving the impression that something very important was about to happen. Then came the fire trucks—more fire trucks than I had ever imagined the base could muster. They came from everywhere and headed for

The XB-70 Valkyrie arrives overhead at Wright-Patterson AFB on the afternoon of February 4, 1969, on its final flight. *Gabriel F. Vacca*

strategic points along the runway. In the distance their blinking lights gave the appearance of dozens of berserk Christmas trees suddenly run amuck.

Finally, as if on cue, a Kaman HH-43B crash rescue helicopter, complete with bright red fire suppression kit hooked to the cargo sling, crept from among the clutter of buildings along the flight line and headed slowly toward the runway at an altitude of no more than 20 feet. After a time it began sidling one way and another, not hovering so much as patrolling.

The tragic loss of the second XB-70 less than three years before, in a midair collision on June 8, 1966, not to mention the earlier cancellation of this $1.5-billion manned supersonic bomber program, had made the Air Force more than a tiny bit touchy whenever the big white experimental bomber gathered media attention. So, Wright-Patterson was on full alert for the arrival of the most spectacular and advanced piece of flying hardware ever to set wheels on its famous runways.

Finally, we spotted something in the sky high over the runway—maybe 8,000 or 10,000 feet. It was a cluster of airplanes at the center of which was a giant, white arrow. The formation flew slowly out of sight to our west toward Dayton and points beyond. Minutes passed before the Valkyrie and her escorts returned. This time they flew directly over our heads, still quite high. My God! One of the escorts was an F-104, the same type of aircraft that had

collided with the number two XB-70, and it was in a position similar to the other F-104 just before the 1966 midair! "Be careful, guys!"

The formation continued on toward the east and disappeared. We saw nothing for close to ten minutes, then suddenly, two miles away at the approach end of the runway there was a cloud of dark smoke and at the head of it was the XB-70, its nose pitched up at an unbelievable angle. (Well, it looked more unbelievable than it really was. We found out later that the pitch angle was nine degrees.) She seemed balanced on that stream of exhaust and continued all the way down the runway at perhaps 100-feet altitude, then climbed a bit and disappeared to the west. Minutes passed. Then again there was the cloud of smoke at the other end of the runway, darker this time, it seemed. The Valkyrie, once more at that seemingly impossible angle of attack, was descending lower and lower toward the runway. So much power! We could hear her now, and almost see the vectors—thrust, lift, gravity, and drag—outlined in the sky tugging and pushing the airplane. Finally, touchdown! Three enormous drag chutes burst out and took hold to help her brakes slow the landing roll. And she rolled and rolled, finally coasting, in one last test of the computerized braking system, all the way to the end of the nearly 2 1/2-mile-long runway, followed all the while by that forest of berserk Christmas trees and the lone HH-43 crash rescue helicopter.

Three of the participants in Valkyrie's last flight: left to right, Donald Mallick, B-58 chase; Lt. Col. Emil "Ted" Sturmthal, XB-70 copilot; and Fitzhugh "Fitz" Fulton, Jr., XB-70 pilot. *Courtesy of Charles R. Frey*

That was it. We'd seen the last flight and landing of the most beautiful, magnificent piece of aeronautical engineering the world had ever known. She was still sitting at the end of the runway, engines running, when we left. Never again would anyone hear that sound. Valkyrie's engines were about to wind down for the last time.

WHERE EAGLES REST

Not long after her last flight, the XB-70 Valkyrie— S/N 62-0001, Air Vehicle-1—was placed on outdoor display at Wright-Patterson's Area C, where the U.S. Air Force Museum was then located, adjacent to the city of Fairborn. She soon became a major attraction, drawing visitors from far and wide to marvel at her mammoth size and stately shape. Here she began her long career as a visual symbol of the museum and as a popular model for amateur and professional photographers alike.

But the XB-70 did not remain in place for very long. In June 1970, construction of a new facility for the museum began at a site about five miles away, on one of Wright Field's now unused runways. In October 1970, well before the new building was completed, the XB-70 and 37 of the museum's other aircraft were moved to the new site. Since most of them were so large that they could neither be economically disassembled and shipped by truck, nor prepared and flown to Wright Field, another method of transportation had to be used. So it was that during three

weekends in October and November 1970, these aircraft were towed off the base from the old museum at Patterson Field, along local and state roads and freeways, to the new museum at Wright Field. The circuitous route covered some eight miles, crossing over load-limited bridges, under height-limiting power lines, and between span-limiting poles and other obstacles.

Moving the XB-70 over this route presented the greatest challenge of all. The Valkyrie's 192-foot length posed the least of the problems in moving her; but the 105-foot wingspan was of great concern. It was necessary to remove and replace poles and signs to allow the aircraft to pass through intersections. Height was also a problem with the twin verticals topping out at almost 31 feet above the ground. The removal of the rudders, which comprised most of the vertical stabilizers, helped considerably. Still, wires and other overhanging obstacles had to be pushed out of the way or temporarily removed.

Weight, however, was probably the most serious limiting factor. The XB-70 had an empty weight of 262,000 pounds, well above the allowable load for the freeway bridge she had to be towed across to reach the new museum site. Removal of the six engines, air conditioning system, and practically everything else that could be taken out reduced the Valkyrie's weight to about 147,000 pounds which was within the design limits of the bridge. Even so, crossing the bridge was a very slow process because the

115

XB-70 AV-1 had been on display at the USAF Museum's aircraft park in Area C on Wright-Patterson AFB since shortly after her arrival on February 4, 1969. Meanwhile, a new Air Force Museum complex was being constructed at the base's Area B, the old Wright Field. Here, Valkyrie is being prepared for her move to her new location. *USAF Museum*

wide tread of the main gear allowed only 8 inches of curb-to-curb clearance, making it an uncomfortably tight squeeze. Eventually, the airplane reached its new parking area and was proudly on display when the newly completed U.S. Air Force Museum facility was dedicated in September 1971.

The XB-70 was destined to remain on outdoor display for another 17 years. Over time she took on the role of U.S. Air Force Museum logo, parked as she was facing the museum's access road. On two occasions she was repainted and each time inspections by the museum's restoration division staff noted some degree of deterioration and delamination. Most notable to the visitor were certain areas on the fuselage and underside that showed evidence of spot delamination of honeycomb skin panels. These were characterized by bubblelike patches on the fuselage aft of the wing apex and similar patches on the bottom of the main center section. Often, visitors would question the appearance of the bubbles but were not always given the correct answers about the delamination by the paid or volunteer staff simply because few people knew what they were.

Whenever the aircraft was stripped and repainted she had to be taken off display and moved to another area

where the work could be done in safety away from the public. When the job was complete, the XB-70 was towed to a special area for update photography, then back to her display area. Each move amounted to a round trip of about two miles. Then, shortly after the museum acquired the Rockwell B-1A (we think of the B-1 as Valkyrie's younger sister), she was again towed to the photography area and posed nose-to-nose with the B-1. Then she was moved back again to her display position in front of the museum.

Those were not the only times the XB-70 was moved because in the year-to-year reposition of outdoor display aircraft, certain readjustments have to be made. But each time that big white experimental bomber was moved, extreme care and a large, heavy-duty tug were required; and at the end, the landing gear had to be positioned on thick steel plates to prevent the wheels from sinking into the tarmac. During one such move, a tire on a main gear wheel caught the sharp edge of one of the steel plates and blew out with an earsplitting explosion. Fortunately, no one was hurt, but those who were nearby said that the sound of a tire pumped to over 200 psi letting go was a real attention-getter.

The delamination process did not begin with the XB-70's retirement to the U.S. Air Force Museum and its

In October 1970, Valkyrie was carefully moved along Wright-Patterson's streets to Ohio's State Route 444. It was a very slow and deliberate process that required the partial closure of the four-lane, limited-access highway. *USAF Museum*

subsequent outdoor display. There is ample evidence to show that some delamination occurred during the flight testing program. It is true, however, that much delamination took place after the airplane was retired to the museum. There are several reasons for this. First, the honeycomb bonding process was not yet fully developed when the first XB-70 entered its test program. Second, after its arrival at Wright-Patterson, the Valkyrie remained on outdoor display, subject to the elements, for some 19 years. Those who were familiar with the XB-70 as displayed were able to see a very gradual deterioration as time went on. Museum management was well aware of the problem and, for that reason, long-range planning had decreed that when the museum's second major exhibits building—eventually dubbed the Modern Flight Hangar—was completed in 1988, the XB-70 would be displayed there, out of the elements. That did happen and, as expected, indoor display of the airplane completely arrested the delamination problem.

Before the Modern Flight Hangar could be opened to the public, a great deal of preparation and shuffling of aircraft took place. Among the larger aircraft to be moved into the building were the C-124, B-52, and B-47. At one point, before she went into the Modern Flight Hangar, the XB-70 was towed to the restoration hangar for some routine maintenance. As the airplane entered the restoration hangar, the movement crew was startled by a loud bang, followed by the appearance of several metal shards falling from the nose gear well. After giving the area a cursory inspection, the crew concluded that a metal conduit support had fractured but posed no structural integrity problem.

Eventually, the Valkyrie was towed into the north end of the display hangar nose first. On the first attempt it was discovered that her twin tails were about two inches too tall to clear the hangar door opening. Rather than resort to the removal of the vertical tails, the restoration crew doing the moving found a simpler solution: deflate the main gear struts and fully inflate the nose gear strut. That pushed up the nose and lowered the tail, which allowed more than an inch of tail clearance to tow the airplane into display position.

Over the next couple of years, the XB-70 was temporarily moved outdoors several times so that additional aircraft could be pulled into the Modern Flight Hangar. Always, she was returned to her prominent display area in the north end of the hangar. Interestingly enough, after the airplane was safely installed in the Modern Flight Hangar, several groups of XB-70 buffs suddenly became interested in her state of preservation and began to flood the museum with their expressions of concern. Since they had not been

The tow vehicle is carefully maneuvering the Valkyrie as the movement crew begins alignment for the approach to the State Route 444 bridge. *USAF Museum*

given a coherent explanation of the delamination problem, many were concerned that the 80-plus-foot nose section of the airplane was going to fall off onto the floor. One "expert" suggested that we put a sling around the nose and tie it to one of the girders supporting the roof of the Modern Flight Hangar. The first problem with that suggestion was that the XB-70's nose was in no danger of falling off. The other problem was that the nose section weighed many times more than the 10,000-pound hanging load capacity of the roof girders. The fact is, and was, that the honeycomb construction is extremely strong and a few flaws would not be significant. Besides, the AV-1 had only the first in a series of refinements of the honeycomb construction processes. No, the Valkyrie was absolutely not going to come apart despite a few popped lamination bonds.

Years of outdoor display and miles of towing for one reason or another had caused a great deal of wear and tear on the Valkyrie's tires. While they were designed to wear through several layers of cord before being replaced, those tires were not best suited for long-term outdoor display, and especially not for the additional wear imposed by the few souvenir-hunting visitors who stripped cord and chunks of rubber from them. Not long after the XB-70 moved indoors, all 10 tires were replaced with a set of spares received with the airplane. Each tire was filled with a urethane rubber compound to eliminate the need to service them regularly with high-pressure air. This "tire-fill" system

worked well with most other museum display aircraft and vehicle tires and has served well in the Valkyrie's case.

In 1992, the U.S. Air Force Museum was to receive a temporary exhibit of former Soviet space hardware. This was a very large exhibit and would require more than the 20,000 square feet occupied by the XB-70. Plans were made to remove the airplane from the Modern Flight Hangar and put her back outdoors for the six or eight months the Soviet Space Exhibit would be in place. Just prior to moving the XB-70 out of the hangar, however, the nose gear well area (where the supposedly fractured conduit support had been noted several years earlier) was given another inspection. This time the inspection uncovered a chilling flaw. One end of a bracket to which the nose gear drag strut was attached was found to be broken. Aircraft structures people who looked at the damage believed that any further movement of the XB-70 might result in collapse of the nose gear. It was, in fact, a minor miracle that the gear had not collapsed during one of the earlier moves. Immediately, a jack pad was affixed to the fuselage jack point forward of the wing apex, and a large hydraulic jack stand was put in place. Other airplanes would make way for the Soviet Space Exhibit, but the Valkyrie could not be moved again until repairs were made. The repairs were to take nearly a year. Meanwhile, the jack under the XB-70's forward fuselage was turned into a display item with the addition of a mannequin clad in a North American maintenance technician's coveralls.

Valkyrie and tow vehicle entering the approach ramp to the bridge. The main landing gear would have a mere 8-inch clearance from the curb while crossing the bridge. *USAF Museum*

The XB-70 leans to the right as she is towed, with only an eight-inch curb-to-main landing gear clearance, across the Route 444 bridge over Mad River. All six YJ-93 engines had to be removed so that Ohio's highway engineers could be satisfied that the airplane would not exceed the bridge's weight limitation. USAF *Museum*

The XB-70 looms over the X-10 as they are both towed toward the USAF Museum. It almost appears as if the Valkyrie is herding her "puppy" along the road in front of her. *USAF Museum*

After leaving Route 444, Valkyrie had to pass through the Village of Riverside on her way to the USAF Museum. Here, like any other road-going vehicle passing through town, she appears to pause at a traffic light before continuing her journey to the museum. Actually, the traffic lights and supporting poles had to give way for her passage rather than the other way around. *USAF Museum*

The XB-70 finally parked at her destination in front of the USAF Museum after the move. She was on outdoor display for nearly 18 years before being moved to inside display in the Modern Flight Hangar. *Jim Benedict*

In the mid-1980s the XB-70 underwent a complete stripping and repainting. In this rare photo she is shown stripped of all but a few patches of her white paint. *Gabriel F. Vacca*

In time, the broken bracket was removed, measured, and duplicated. The new bracket was check fitted, then heat treated, and finally reinstalled. Although the new bracket was not officially airworthy, it was said by its replicators to be stronger than the original and able to take the stresses of towing. Interestingly enough, the Valkyrie was not moved for nearly five years after the repair.

Toward the end of 1997, however, there was some talk of moving the XB-70 to the Research and Development Hangar (formerly the Museum's Annex South) on the old Wright Field flight line. Whether the airplane would suffer any other damage from another mile or so of towing is anyone's guess. One can only hope that there will be no repeat of the several near-catastrophic main gear failures experienced when the aircraft was still actively being flight tested back in the 1960s.

CHAPTER 11

Epilogue

At the North American Aviation (NAA) plant in Palmdale, California, back in the early 1960s, a group of executives gathered around their latest creation, the XB-70 "Valkyrie." She was a magnificent sight. The NAA working crews and management were proud of her. They were also proud because the secretary of defense, Robert Strange McNamara, was on his way to visit the plant and look at their latest creation. They waited, and they were anxious. Everything they had worked for rested on the secretary's visit to the plant. At stake was everything they had brought to fruition in the technological marvel of the two XB-70 prototypes.

Finally, Secretary McNamara's car drove up. Everyone waited to greet him, but the secretary apparently wasn't interested in polite greetings. He exited his car, and in his best Whiz Kid fashion, took a short walk around the XB-70, got back into his car, and drove off. What an anticlimax! Not only were the people of NAA left to wonder what they had done to deserve such cavalier treatment, but they were also left wondering about the very future of the XB-70.

An old *Life* magazine article describes how literally thousands of hearts were broken when the XB-70 was canceled. Was this claim merely an exaggeration? How could it possibly be true? Skepticism evaporates when you consider McNamara's disdainfully brief visit. It seems that after 35 years, the pain and sense of loss still remains. To be sure, programs get canceled every day, but this was different. McNamara's visit provides focus on the real reason the XB-70 was canceled. It was not because of funding shortages. It was not because she wasn't a viable design. And it was not because of insurmountable technical problems. The main reason the airplane was canceled was because of the bean-counter mentality rampant in the Department of Defense at the time. The only things that mattered to McNamara were statistics. If the numbers didn't add up, scrap the project.

The case of the XB-70 was "all or nothing." Most of the time if it wasn't to Secretary McNamara's liking, it was "nothing." No one knew better how to manipulate figures to prove a point, and as long as he controlled that point, he couldn't lose. The people of the United States, the U.S. Air Force, the producers of the XB-70, and the world of aviation found this out too late.

The people who put their hearts, souls, intelligence, blood, and, in one instance, their very lives into the development of the XB-70 needed to have the story told. Valkyrie herself, at the U.S. Air Force Museum, needs to be recognized as a monument to the people who developed her, the technological advances she supplied, and not stand merely as the lone survivor of a program waylaid largely because of political ambition and pride. Nonetheless, because of the XB-70's cancellation, the United States has had to "reinvent the wheel" and redo much of what was in progress or already done by the people in the Valkyrie program.

Flying accidents are often rooted in bureaucratic expediency and lack of communication. Both the XB-70 AV-2 accident, and the tragic loss of the space shuttle *Challenger* 20 years later, likely stemmed from an overly emphasized "Can do!" attitude. Was *Challenger's* demise just bad luck? No. *Challenger* died because of a lack of communication at launch time. It was similar to the lack of communication that existed before the XB-70 AV-2 accident. A close formation was not planned on the day of the accident flight. Critical warning signals were missed in both cases. The concept of "acceptable risk," perhaps too liberally applied, flawed the decision-making process.

A tangle of paperwork teamed with undocumented verbal instructions, often help expedite an agenda. Unfortunately there can be tragic consequences. In 1966, it took the loss of two pilots, an expensive aircraft, and a valuable test program. In 1986, it took the destruction of an Orbiter and seven lives to rectify what should have been fixed many years before.

Since 1966, many practices have been changed as a result of these tragedies. But America's bureaucracy continues to ax important programs, and aerospace research and development suffers. America's lack of a shuttle replacement, supersonic transport, or a space station can be traced back to programs that were canceled, leaving us to start over and develop them again. Reinventing the wheel? How much has *really* changed?

Escorted by an F-104, XB-70 Valkyrie #20001 lands at Wright-Patterson AFB at the end of her last flight, February 4, 1969. USAF Museum

BIBLIOGRAPHY

Air Force Headquarters Air Research and Development, Vol III. Washington, D.C.: Office of Air Force History, Jan. 1, 1959.

Air Force Magazine. Air Force Association, Arlington, VA.

Anderson, Jack. "Coming: The B-70 Jet; It's Half Plane, Half Spaceship." *Parade Magazine,* July 1958.

Apple, Nick P., and Gene Gurney. *The Air Force Museum.* Dayton, OH: The Central Printing Company, 1991.

Aviation Week & Space Technology. McGraw-Hill Companies, New York, NY.

B-70 Program Status Report, USAF/SC, November 2, 1961.

B-70 Strategic Bomber Prototype Configuration, North American Aviation, Los Angeles, CA, January 11, 1960.

Beschloss, Michael R. *Mayday: Eisenhower and the U-2 Affair.* New York: Harper Row, 1986.

Bottom, Edgar. *Balance of Terror (Nuclear Weapons and the Illusion of Security, 1945-1985).* Boston: Brown Press, 1986.

Briggs, B. Bruce. *Shield of Faith.* New York: Simon and Schuster, 1988.

Brugioni, Dino. *Eyeball to Eyeball.* New York: Random House, 1991.

Bundy, McGeorge. *Danger and Survival—Choices about the Bomb in the First 50 Years.* New York: Random House, 1988.

Burrows, William E. *Deep Black.* New York: Berkeley Books, 1986.

Byrne, John A. *The Whiz Kids: Ten Founding Fathers of American Business—and the Legacy They Left Us.* New York: Currency Doubleday, 1993.

Campbell, Joseph. *Primitive Mythology: The Masks of God.* New York: Penguin Books, 1969.

Coffey, Thomas M. *Iron Eagle: The Turbulent Life of General Curtis LeMay.* New York: Crown Publishers, 1986.

Cotterell, Arthur. *World Mythology.* Oxford, England: Oxford Press, 1986.

Cresswell, Mary Ann, and Carl Berger. *United States Air Force History: An Annotated Bibliography.* Washington, D.C.: Office of Air Force History, 1971.

Crossley-Holland, Kevin, *The Norse Myths.* New York: Pantheon Books, 1980.

Dalquest, Leonard A., Eric R. Falk, et al., ed. *Seven Decades of Progress: A Heritage of Aircraft Turbine Technology.* Fallbrook, CA: Aero Publishers, 1979.

Developmental Program Manual, XB-70A (Propulsion System), USAF, July 30, 1966.

Development of Airborne Armament, 1910-1961, (Historical Study) Historical Division, Office of Information, Aeronautical Systems Division (Air Force Systems Command), Wright-Patterson AFB, OH, October 1961.

Donaldson, Bruce K. *Analysis of Aircraft Structure.* New York: McGraw-Hill, 1990.

Donaldson, Robert T., M.D. "Aeromedical Aspects of the XB-70 Aircraft" paper. USAF Museum Research Div/Wright Patterson AFB, OH, February 1964.

Foxworth, Thomas G. "North American XB-70: Half Airplane—Half Spacecraft." *Historical Aviation Album,* 1969.

Francillon, Rene' J. *Lockheed Aircraft Since 1913.* Annapolis, MD: Naval Institute Press, 1987.

Freschel, Edward, Jr., and Elbert S. Steel. "Development of the XB-70 Propulsion System." *North American Aviation,* Los Angeles, CA, November 1965.

Fulton, Fitzhugh, Jr. "Lessons from the XB-70 as Applied to the Supersonic Transport." NASA Flight Research Center, Edwards AFB, CA, October 1968 (American Institute of Aeronautics and Astronautics).

Ground Support Equipment, North American Aviation, Los Angeles, CA, 1960.

Hamilton, Edith. *Mythology.* Boston: Little Brown and Company, 1942.

Hendrickson, Paul. *The Living and the Dead.* New York: Knopf, 1997.

Herf, Jeffery. *War by Other Means.* New York: Free Press/MacMillian Press, 1991.

Holder, W. G. *B-1 Bomber.* 2d ed., vol. 35. Blue Ridge, PA: Aero Books, 1985.

Hoopes, Townsend, and Douglas Brinkley. *Driven Patriot: The Life and Times of James Forrestal.* New York: Vintage Press, 1992.

Horwitch, Mel. *Clipped Wings: the American SST Conflict.* Cambridge, MA: MIT Press, 1982.

Kaku, Michio, and David Axelrod. *To Win a Nuclear War: The Pentagon's Secret War Plans.* Boston: South End Press, 1987.

Kaufman, Richard. *The War Profiteers.* Indianapolis: Bobbs Merril Press, 1970.

Kent, Richard, Jr. *Safe, Secure, and Soaring—A History of the Federal Civil Aviation Administration Policy—1961-1972,* Washington, D.C.: U.S. Department of Transportation, 1980.

LeMay, Gen. Curtis E., with MacKinlay Kantor. *Mission with LeMay: My Story.* Garden City, NY: Doubleday & Company, 1965.

LeMay, Gen. Curtis E., and Maj. Gen. Dale O. Smith. *America Is in Danger.* New York: Funk & Wagnalls, 1968.

Mason, Herbert Molloy, Jr. *The United States Air Force: A Turbulent History.* New York: Mason/Carter, 1976.

McDonnell, Malcolm. *Challenger: A Major Malfunction.* Garden City, NY: Doubleday, 1987.

McDougall, Walter A. *The Heavens and the Earth: A Political History of Space.* New York: Basic Books, 1988.

McMaster, H.R. *Dereliction of Duty.* New York: Harper Collins, 1997.

McNamara, Robert S. *Blundering into Disaster: Surviving the first century of the Nuclear Age.* New York: Pantheon Books, 1986.

McNamara, Robert S., with Brian VanDeMark. *In Retrospect: The Tragedy and Lessons of Vietnam.* New York: Times Books, 1995.

McNamara, Robert S. *The Essence of Security: Reflections in Office.* New York: Harper and Row, 1968.

McNaughton, Thomas L. *New Weapons-Old Politics: America's Procurement Muddle.* Washington DC: Brookings Institution, 1989.

Memorandum for the Secretary of Defense "XB-70 Investigation," Department of the Air Force, Washington, D.C., August 12, 1966.

Miller, Jay. *Lockheed Martin's Skunk Works.* Leicester, England: Midland Publishing, 1995.

Moon, Howard. *Soviet SST: The Techno-politics of the Tupolev-144.* New York: Orion Books, 1989.

Morris, Charles. *Iron Destinies/ Lost Opportunities: The Arms Race Between the USA and the USSR 1945-1987.* New York: Harper Row, 1988.

Neufeld, Jacob. *The Development of Ballistic Missiles in the United States Air Force, 1945-1960.* Washington, D.C.: Office of Air Force History, 1990.

Newhouse, John. *War and Peace in the Nuclear Age.* New York: Knopf Press, 1984.

Newman, John M. *JFK and Vietnam.* Warner Books, 1996.

Page, R. I. *Norse Myths.* University of Texas Press, 1990.

Peebles, Curtis. *Dark Eagles: A History of Top Secret U.S. Aircraft Programs.* Novato, CA: Presidio Press, 1995.

Pike, Iain. "B-70: State-of-the-Art Improver/Part I." *Flight International*, June 25, 1964.

Public Papers of the Presidents—John F. Kennedy, 1961-1963. Washington, D.C.: U.S. Government Printing Office, 1963.

Rees, Ed. *The Manned Missile: The Story of the B-70.* New York: Duell, Sloan and Pearce, 1960.

Reinsch, Wayne A. North American Aviation, "Titanium Fabrication Technique for the XB-70 and Beyond." Society of Automotive Engineers, Aeronautics Space Engineering and Manufacturing Meeting, Los Angeles, CA, October 3-7, 1966.

Report to the President by the Presidential Commission on the Space Shuttle *Challenger* Accident, vols. I through V. Washington, D.C.: NASA, February 26, 1986–May 2, 1986.

Reymal, Kenneth. *Rapier: North American's F-108A.* undated. USAF Museum Research Division/Wright Patterson AFB, undated.

Rich, Ben R., and Leo Janos. *Skunk Works: A Personal Memoir of My Years at Lockheed.* Boston: Little, Brown and Company, 1994.

Ross, J. W., and D. B. Rogerson. *Aircraft Prototype and Technology Demonstration Symposium: XB-70 Technology Advancements, North American Aviation Operations,* American Institute of Aeronautics and Astronautics, March 23-24, 1983.

Scheslinger, Arthur. *A Thousand Days: John F. Kennedy in the White House.* Cambridge, MA: Riverside Press/Houghton-Mifflin Co., 1965.

Schilling, Hammond, and Snyder. *Strategy, Politics and Defense Budgets.* New York: Columbia University Press, 1962.

Shapley, Deborah. *Promise and Power: The Life and Times of Robert McNamara.* Boston: Little, Brown and Company, 1993.

Sherman, Dennis March. "The National Security Act: A Blueprint for the Congressional Role in Weapons Development." (A Case Study of the B-70 Bomber Program.) Madison, WI: University of Wisconsin, 1978.

Sturlerson, Snori. *Eddas.* London/Vermont: Everyman Press, 1987.

Swanborough, Gordon and Peter M. Bowers. *United States Military Aircraft Since 1909,* Smithsonian Institution Press, Washington, D.C., 1989.

Sweetman, Bill. *Northrop B-2 Stealth Bomber.* Osceola, WI: Motorbooks International, 1992.

Sweetman, Bill, and James Goddall. *Lockheed F-117A: Operation and Development of the Stealth Fighter.* Osceola, WI: Motorbooks International, 1990.

Thayer, J. *Air Transport Policy and National Security.* Chapel Hill: University of North Carolina Press, 1965.

Trento, Joseph J. *Prescription for Disaster: From the Glory to the Betrayal of the Shuttle.* New York: Crown Publications, 1987.

USAF Accident/Incident Report, USAF Mishap Report, and Accident Board Proceedings concerning loss of XB-70 #20207 and F-104 #813, 8 June 1966, with multiple attachments (181 pages).

Vaughan, Diane. *The Challenger Launch Decision.* Chicago: University of Chicago Press, 1996.

Walker, Lois E., and Shelby E. Wickam. *From Huffman Prairie to the Moon: The History of Wright-Patterson Air Force Base.* Hq. Wright-Patterson AFB, OH: Air Force Logistics Command, 1985.

Watson, George M. *The Office of the Secretary of the Air Force, 1947-1965.* Washington, D.C.: Center for Air Force History, 1993.

Wheeler, Keith. "The Full Story of the 28 Seconds That Killed the XB-70." *Life Magazine*, November 11, 1966.

Wise, David, and Thomas B. Ross. *The U-2 Affair.* New York: Random House, 1962.

Wolf, Richard I., comp. *The United States Air Force: Basic Documents on Roles and Missions.* (Air Staff Historical Study.) Washington, D.C.: Office of Air Force History, 1987.

XB-70 Program Study (WS110A), Air Force Logistics Command Office of History, Wright-Patterson AFB, OH , February 3, 1964.

Yeager, Gen. Chuck, and Leo Janos. *Yeager: An Autobiography.* New York: Bantam Books, 1985.

York, Herbert F. *Making Weapons, Talking Peace: A Physicist's Odyssey from Hiroshima to Geneva.* New York: Basic Books, 1987.

York, Herbert F. *Race to Oblivion.* New York: Simon and Shuster, 1970.

Index